ARDMORE:
Home, Community and Golf

by
Wallace George du Temple
and
Co-Authored
by
Edward R. Ostachowicz

ISBN
978-1-77097-750-1 (Paperback)

Published by:

FriesenPress
Suite 300 – 852 Fort Street
Victoria, BC, Canada V8W 1H8

www.friesenpress.com

Distributed to the trade by The Ingram Book Company

Ardmore: Community, Home and Golf

This book has been co-authored by Edward R.Ostachowicz, and Wallace George du Temple. Golf Club information was researched and written by Edward R. Ostachowicz. All data used was taken from recorded meetings, events, and dialogue with long-time members.

The history of the origins of Ardmore and of golf in North Saanich was researched by Wallace G. du Temple. All data used was taken from recorded meetings, events, dialogue with longtime members, personal diaries and memoirs, newspaper articles, audio recordings from the Provincial Archives, electronic files, web-pages and records from the Saanich Pioneers' Society and the Sidney Archives.

All printing costs to produce the book have been paid for by 'Bunti Holdings Ltd'. Any monetary gains that may be acquired from the sale of this book will be paid to the 'Ardmore Golf Club'. The revenue is to be shared equally by the Parent, Men's, & Ladies Divisions.

Don Delaney photographed birds for several seasons at Ardmore Golf Club. He created a slide show entitled, "Birds Over Ardmore". We thank him sincerely for the right to use many of these images within the manuscript. Ardmore Golf Course is proud of its environmental stewardship that has enhanced the property as a bird sanctuary

Thanks to all who contributed in this endeavor!

The Ardmore Oak Tree was a symbol of the golf course and the family.

I painted the "Oak Tree" as a special gift for my Mom, (Betty (Du Temple) Snobelen), not knowing that they would both be gone within 10 years. Hopefully this painting will last forever as a remembrance of our family and the Ardmore Oak Tree.

Penny (Du Temple) Baziuk

Penny holds the course records at: Glen Meadows, Desert Willow Mountainview, Desert Willow Firecliff, Cordova Bay, and Indian Canyons (all from the red tees).

One of the highlights of Penny's golf career was being on the 2007 Provincial Team that represented BC in the Canadian Senior Amateur. Penny placed 2nd during the 2010 Canadian Mid Masters and 4th in the Mid Amateur.

Penny won the Zone Championship in 2004 as an amateur and 2010 as a senior.

Penny (Du Temple) Baziuk has won the WSCGA Div II Seniors 5 years in a row.

The Du Temple family and Ardmore Golf Course claim Penny (Du Temple) Baziuk as their very own, the best Ardmore golfer and the best ambassador for Ardmore Golf Course.

Table of Contents

Introduction

On a stormy night in October 1904 flames arose abruptly on the west side of the Ardmore Manor House of Lord William Le Poer Trench the site of the first Ardmore Golf Course. In hellish flames the most magnificent Edwardian home of Vancouver Island and Ardmore was 'gone with the wind'. From the native long house in Cole Bay, the Salish could see the two story English mansion burning. The flames licked the sky as tall firs caught fire and then crowned. The westerly gusts drove sparks and burning embers into the fall night.

The First Great Fire in North Saanich. The Manor House Burns. This is a simulation of the historic fire provided by N.S. Fire Chief, Gary Wilkins.

William Le Poer Trench, member of the British House of Lords, owner of all that is Ardmore today, with family and servants fled from the blaze and huddled on the first tee of Ardmore Golf Course. Arson was suspected because of the very sudden start of the conflagration. Blame was directed towards the First Peoples in Cole Bay whose dogs had been shot by the Lord. Was it retaliation for that? Had the blaze been an accident?

Hon Le Poer / Lord of Ardmore Hon. William Le Poer Trench

The Lord left the country almost immediately, sold Ardmore to a land developer, and returned to the old country. Had he fled in fear for his life? Had he returned to Britain because there primogeniture, privilege, and class structure still flourished but was not properly respected in Ardmore? Had he yearned for his social contacts with the lines of aristocrats who ruled the British estates, the deference of the discreet servants, and the social structures that kept them apart. Certainly he had suffered dreadfully since the upstairs-downstairs life of the inhabitants of the great English Manor Houses could not be imitated in Ardmore. In England one aristocratic family could have an army of up to three hundred servants. Drapery alone in a Manor House could be worth millions while a kitchen maid, one of the lower echelons of the house's servants made the equivalent of twenty-five dollars in a year.

"Ardmore: Community, Home and Golf" is a book about Ardmore as a place on the Saanich Peninsula. It is also about suspicion of arson, about scandal, racism, farming, residential development, the Du Temple family and the early days of golfing on Vancouver Island.

The story of Ardmore as a place begins further back in the olden times.

Chapter One:

The Geological History of Ardmore

We will begin by explaining how Ardmore was formed geologically and in so doing refer to the studies of seismologists.

Ardmore appears peaceful and bucolic today but the land was created by a cataclysmic creation process of earthquakes and explosive volcanoes that went on for more than sixty thousand years. Vancouver Island was once far to the southwest in the Pacific Ocean. It slid gradually northeast on the Pacific Plate until the largest of the archipelagos – Wrengellia – collided about ninety million years ago with ancient North America, which was moving slowly southwestward. The collision drove the edge of Wrangellia downward, creating the Georgia Depression, today's Strait of Georgia and Puget Sound.

In this way molten lava had made lovely Ardmore. We all know that Ardmore has a very warm climate in comparison to Canada's other provinces and territories. Residents of those other places have no doubt been on the receiving end of smug New Year's email messages from someone here at Ardmore boasting about daffodils in bloom. In February, news is sent eastward to the frozen hinterland with news of the February flower count.

Well so be it, because science now shows that residents of Ardmore and area might actually be historically justified in their annual bluster. Scientists believe that during the height of the Wisconsin glaciation, the Earth's most recent spell of global cooling or "Ice Age," Ardmore and region was not covered by ice sheets. While most of Canada lay entombed in up to three kilometres of ice, grass grew sweet and tender for roaming herds of imperial mammoths, mastodons, muskoxen, bison and other ice age species where daffodils grow today. Sea levels had lowered because of the fact that a massive amount of water was held in the glacier ice fields that covered the continent. A land bridge and marsh between the peninsula and the mainland allowed migrating animals to seek refuge in Ardmore. Scientists have uncovered skeletal remains of many species on the Peninsula that prove the point. To see them visit the Royal BC Museum at 655 Belleville Street in Victoria B.C.

Violent geological events created Ardmore, but a gigantic flood created the sea floor of Saanich Fjord or Inlet that is one of Ardmore's most notable features. The Saanich Fjord is twenty-one kilometers in length and is remarkably varied. Ardmore's Fjord coastline is graced with pleasant pocket pebble beaches but further south at Finlayson Arm the shore- line becomes steep and craggy. Like many European Fjords, it is deeper inland than at its' mouth. The sediment on its' seabed has an amazing story to tell.

About 11,800 calendar years ago, a catastrophic flood roared down the Fraser Valley, across the Strait of Georgia and into Saanich Inlet. An enormous amount of impounded melt-water broke a natural ice dam in the Thompson Valley. The water surged like a gigantic tsunami down the Fraser River sweeping everything with it and swamped lower parts of the Gulf Islands. It carried trees, wildlife, silt, mud, plants, shrubs and perhaps humans. Because at great depths in the Saanich Inlet little oxygen exists scientists have removed intact specimens from which pollen and DNA has been extracted. These specimens came from

the Thompson River area. Much more remains to be discovered on the sea bottom of the 'Ardmore Fjord'.

There are no written accounts of this devastating flood,
but the evidence is clearly written in the deep clay on the
floor of both the strait and Saanich Inlet. The First Nations,
on whose territory Ardmore resides, have an oral memory
of a great flood from which they sought and found rescue
at the top of Mount Newton or LÁU,WELNEW . It is unclear
whether that memory refers to the ancient Fraser River
flood-tsunami or to the much later earthquake-tsunami
of 1700.

That earthquake sent a tsunami racing across the
Pacific, and the arrival time was noted when the waves
washed ashore in Japan. The Japanese records enabled
researchers to determine that the quake struck off
Ardmore and Vancouver Island at about 9 p.m. on Jan.
26, 1700.

Recent scientific studies confirm that a monster earthquake rivaling these ancient events and the recent one
that devastated Japan in March 2011 is all but a certainty
for Ardmore and North America's Pacific coast.

No one can say when it will occur, but when it does a
huge and powerful wall of water could hit the outer coast
areas within 30 to 45 minutes. A swelling wall of water
will inundate the Vancouver International Airport about an
hour and a half later. Because Ardmore is on the east side
of the Saanich Peninsula, the tsunami will have to sweep
around Oak Bay and through the Haro Strait towards
Vancouver. Players at Ardmore will be able to complete
their golf rounds because all of Ardmore is sufficiently
high as to avoid any eventuality of flooding. Other low-
lying areas of Sidney and North Saanich will be flooded if
the tsunami hits during a high tide.

Yarrow Point Cole Bay, The South Side of Ardmore

Chapter Two

First Nations, First Peoples

First Nations have inhabited Ardmore and region for many centuries. Europeans did not discover Ardmore or the Pacific Coast. They just arrived. It has long been thought that Vancouver Island first came to the attention of Britain after the third voyage of Captain James Cook, who spent a month during 1778 at Nootka Sound on the island's western coast. Cook claimed it for the United Kingdom. However, in "The Secret Voyage of Sir Francis Drake" by Samuel Bawlf an opinion is offered with the proof of old maps that Sir Francis Drake visited the east coast of Vancouver Island and passed close by Ardmore in 1578. He had sailed in the Golden Hind from Dixon Entrance to the Fraser River in the process of tracing the coastal contours of what would become British Columbia. The details of this trip were kept as a state secret. The harbour at Comox was probably the planned strategic site as a home for the British admiralty in its' contest with Spain for supremacy in the Pacific.

Other European mariners to arrive have left traces of their appearance in the names of the islands and water ways we all know: the islands of Vancouver, Galiano, San Quan, Valdes, De Courcy, Gabriola: the waterways of Trincomali Channel, Strait of Georgia, and the Strait of Juan De Fuca.

In recent times the area in which these islands and waterways reside has been renamed as The Salish Sea. The Salish Sea includes the Strait of Juan de Fuca, Strait of Georgia, and Puget Sound, and all their connecting channels and adjoining waters, such as haro Strait, Rosario Strait, and the waters around and between the San Quan Islands. The Salish Sea extends north to Desolation Sound.

Coast Salish is a term that is used to describe the groups of indigenous peoples who live in southwest British Columbia and northwest Washington state along the Salish Sea. They share a common linguistic and cultural origin.

The waterways of the Salish Sea were important trade routes for the Coast Salish when the settlers arrived and they remain a source of food and other resources for the indigenous peoples.

By the time the colony of Vancouver Island was established in 1849, British administrators had developed a colonial policy that recognized aboriginal possession of land. In 1850 the Hudson's Bay Company, which was responsible for British settlement of Vancouver Island as part of its trading license agreement with the Crown, began purchasing lands for colonial settlement and industry from aboriginal peoples on Vancouver Island.

Between 1850 and 1854, James Douglas, as chief factor of Fort Victoria and governor of the colony, made a series of fourteen land purchases from aboriginal peoples. The Douglas Treaties cover approximately 358 square miles of land around Victoria, Saanich, Sooke, Nanaimo and Port Hardy, all on Vancouver Island.

Treaty negotiations by Douglas did not continue beyond 1854 due, in part, to a lack of funds and the slow progress of settlement and industry in the 1850s.

Douglas' policies toward aboriginal peoples and land were generally consistent with British principles. Those of his political successors, however, proved to be not as consistent.

The fourteen Douglas treaties are similar in approach. An area of land was surrendered "entirely and forever" in exchange for cash, clothing, or blankets. The signatories and their descendants retained existing village sites and fields for their continued use, the "liberty to hunt over unoccupied lands" and the right to "carry on their fisheries as formerly."

Douglas' land purchases have consistently been upheld as treaties by the courts (R. v. White and Bob, 1964; R. v. Bartleman, 1984; Claxton v. Saanichton Marina Ltd., 1989). In 1987 the Tsawout Band successfully obtained a permanent injunction restraining the construction of a marina in Saanichton Bay on the grounds that the proposed facility

Patricia Bay and The Airport, The North Side of Ardmore

would interfere with fishing rights promised to them by their 1852 treaty.

When 'Klee Wyck' authored by Emily Carr was published in 1941 an era of contradictions continued. Emily Carr used her eloquent and touching combination of words to cause a sharp twinge of conscience in the reader. She showed in words and paintings that so-called white and missionary "progress" was destroying the natural beauty and ways of a fine people. However, a paternalistic federal government continued its anti-potlatching legislation and other measures to deprive First Nations of their traditions and culture, and to assimilate them into settler society. Yet small non-Native organizations were springing up to counter the prevailing opinion. Some Ardmore

golfers were members of the B.C. Indian Arts and Welfare Society, which promoted cross-cultural understanding and awareness, encouraging artists to continue and pass on their traditions to the next generations. At the same time in the schools native children were forbidden to speak their Native languages or follow traditional ways. The physical, sexual and psychological abuse was extensive. It was a shameful time of contradictions.

Today many people honour and respect First Nations and seek to be partners with them for a co-operative and sustainable future. The negative effects attributed to the abusive policies of government are gradually being over-come by the perseverance of a proud people, by attempts at reconciliation and by impressive language revival pro-grams. However, the past is like a southwesterly storm that has knocked down trees and branches, over-turned sheds and torn up roof tops, drowned canoes and before repairs can be done another one hits.

SENĆOŦEN (pronounced sen-chaw-sen) as a language was developed organically over thousands of years, and holds a very intimate and very tangible, connection to these lands. Uvic's Lorna Williams explains, that the sounds expressed in SENĆOŦEN come from the wind, from the water, from the trees, from plants and from the ancestors. Many of the words have no equivalent in English.

Before Europeans' contact SENĆOŦEN, which means "Saanich Talk," was spread by trade and intermarriage across the Georgia Strait to Tsawwassen, the Olympic Peninsula, and the nearby Gulf Islands. On the Peninsula it was the dominant language, with perhaps 7,000 speakers here in 1852. European diseases decimated that popula-tion. Discriminatory language policies sought to destroy the language. Thanks to the work of proud elders the lan-guage is having a revival.

From about 1999 a strong group of Salish people have joined Ardmore Golf Course and some have become loyal employees. Mr. Paul Sam, senior, is a SENĆOŦEN language teacher at the LÁU,WELNEW Tribal School and an organizer of First Nations Golf Tournaments at Ardmore. I have tried with my limited knowledge to show respect and give thanks to our Salish neighbours for sharing this land of Ardmore with us. I recognize that problems from the past still exist. If we compare the housing in Ardmore to the housing in Tseycum or Pauquachin who can not see the disparity? Acts of colonialism resulted in the difficult conditions First Nations face today. Sylvia Olsen wrote recently in the Seaside Times, "When one people superimposes its society on another and systematically excludes the original people from wealth-making opportunities then it follows that there will be vast inequality and social disruption. A further important question is why have the inequalities lasted so long? Housing is a good example. First Nations people make very few of the important decisions about how reserve housing is delivered to their communities... There are no easy answers but there is a better approach. Let people speak for themselves and act on their own behalf."

Heart of Ardmore

Chapter Three

Surrey Ride Around the District of North Saanich in 1891

What was Ardmore and the District of North Saanich like in those early days? Let us reference an article that appeared in the June 20th issue of the Review written by G.E.J., W.H.R. and J.J.W. that was entitled "Enjoy A Thrilling Surrey Ride Around This District in 1891."This was the year that the town site of Sidney was established.

There were less than 40 farmers' home-sites in the whole of North Saanich in 1891 and very few other buildings, except for the most magnificent estate of William Le Poer Trench.

The district supported two churches, the Holy Trinity Anglican Church at Union Bay, now called Pat Bay, and the Methodist Church at the junction of East Saanich and Mills Roads. All the children had to walk to school between the two churches on Mills Road. There were lots of cabins in the district occupied by bachelors who, for the most part, worked for the farmers. Several single men were fishermen, and others were loggers and wood workers. Many of the larger farms started inland and then continued down to the sea. Mt Newton stood in the middle of the countryside. Four years later on October 2nd, 1895 John Dean would purchase acreage on Mt Newton that he would later donate to the province as a park.

"Jump in my surrey and come for a ride," writes J.J. White one of the first golfers in Ardmore. Starting at the southern boundary of North Saanich, on the East Saanich

Road, we traverse an interesting and twisting bit of road that brings us to one of the finest views, unsurpassed anywhere, the Experimental Farm Hill. Notice the glimpses here and there through the trees of the Olympic Range of mountains to the south and the Mount Baker group to the east. We are fortunate today, as there are now clouds to hide Mount Rainier to the southeast. Take special note of Mount Waddington to the north, the tip of which is just visible to the right of Mount Tuam on Salt Spring Island. As we turn our gaze to the surrounding woods, enjoy the beauty of the dogwood trees, now in full bloom.

Bird Ponds at Ardmore

When we climb up Mount Newton on our left, we look out in all directions and see a complete circle of beautiful mountains and waterways. In season we would walk past wild flowers such as Sea Brush, Camas, Shooting Stars, Spring Gold, and Fairy Slipper while in the air and trees Ravens, Eagles, Woodpeckers, Wrens, and Hummingbirds busily work their wings and feathers in the life of the forest.

As the carriage moves ahead over the uneven track we would see the early pioneers plowing and cultivating, harvesting and threshing. We would see animals grazing in the fields, or birds rising up from hedgerows when disturbed by the approaching carriage. Farmers are nurturing their orchards. The fruit trees produce bushels of peaches, pears, apples, plums, apricots and cherries on laden branches. Apart from the fruit trees, notice the luscious red strawberries, loganberries, raspberries and blackberries trained on what seems like miles of wire.

The carriage tour takes us from Mt Newton, past the 1000 acre farm of bachelors William and Charles Ray, the five farms of the Brethour brothers, the farms of J. T. McIlmoyl and Peter Imrie, near School Cross Road that would become Mills Cross Road; past the three farms of Samuel Roberts: past Shoal Harbour and the old Wright's Hotel and post office to Wains Road and to the holdings of Mr. Ruffus P. Horth. Mr. Horth had the stagecoach business and had the mail contract to Victoria. He was one of the first hop growers in the district.

At the junction of Wain Road and West Saanich the surrey ride brings us to farm of Henry Wain and the 500 acre farm of D.D. Moses. Turning left off of Wains Road

Bird Habitat

onto West Saanich, the surrey is on the way to the farm of William Towner that lies on the right. The Towner home is on the corner of this road and we are greeted with an unusual sight, for here we see two large hop kilns in a field of growing hops, a thriving industry in that day.

Exotic Trees at Ardmore

Were we to enter an unplowed portion of a farmers' property we would no doubt see areas carpeted with wild flowers, ranging from minute pansies and clovers to the infinitely more conspicuous and dramatic tiger lilies and great patches of Indian paintbrushes in their vivid reds and oranges.

As we drive along on our journey we leave the Towner property on our right and the Caswell on our left, as we come to Union Bay, later to be called Pat Bay, and the Tsecum native community. If we look across the bay, we see the Malahat, Saanich Arm and further west, the snow-capped peaks of the Vancouver Island Mountains. Next we come to Meadlands Farm.

Lets take a minute to walk down to a beach on the Saanich Inlet. As we descend we notice rock plants with white or yellow blooms between the granite out-crops where soil resides. We might see honeysuckle vines circling some of the trees with brilliant clusters of orange trumpets.

Amphibian Paradise at Ardmore

At the beach we would see crabs of all sorts and sizes scuttling across the sand while close by are sea cucumbers and sea urchins. The display of starfish, purple, and orange does not go unnoticed as they overlap each other in motionless mounds while waiting for the Salish Sea to return. The stranded sea anemones display pink centres that look like pimento stuffed olives.

Back in the carriage the horses pull us south on West Saanich until we reach the properties of George Mills, and Holy Trinity Church. Mr. Mills gifted the land, two acres in extent, for the erection of the church and parsonage. The church was built by pioneer cooperation and generosity, with lumber especially milled and floated over from Genoa Bay. The church was solemnly set apart for sacred uses, and dedicated to "the Holy and Undivided Trinity" on June 27th, 1885.

Further south we reach the beautiful wooded area of Ardmore with the Ardmore Farm to both the east and west side of the West Saanich Road. Here is the property and mansion of the British Lord, William Le Poer Trench, whose estate with tennis courts and golf course, the Ardmore Golf Course, stands out in contrast to the pioneer farms round about.

The William Le Poer mansion at Ardmore was magnificent. The prominent features of its' imposing structure were the expansive roof with large front gable and bracketing, finials, stone base and tapered columns to the roofline. The exterior of the house was clad in drop siding and the gabling and dormers were shingled.

Inside, there was a tasteful use of dark wood paneling and many evidences of good and careful construction. Ships had brought Edwardian furnishings for the parlor. The walls were made of tongue-and-grove lumber. Kerosene lamps would have been placed here and there for nighttime convenience. From the ceiling glass icicles dangled and sparkled below a central hanging oil lamp. Above the huge fireplace, with granite hearth and oak mantle, hickory golf clubs from the old country were displayed. A small organ occupied one part of the room and every couch and chair flaunted an array of hand-embroidered cushions in a profusion of colours.

Lord Le Poer Trench had insisted on having a games room on the main floor that held all of the necessary sporting equipment for golf, tennis, lawn bowling, shooting, and crocket.

A grand stairway led up to bedrooms with unobstructed views of Cole Bay. At the very front of the second story there was an observation porch from which ships coming into Cole Bay could be observed through a fixed spyglass. To the east of the main residence and close to West Saanich Road stood a two-story gatekeepers home. An impressive ornate steel gate held by two high granite posts guarded the entrance and carriage path to the livery

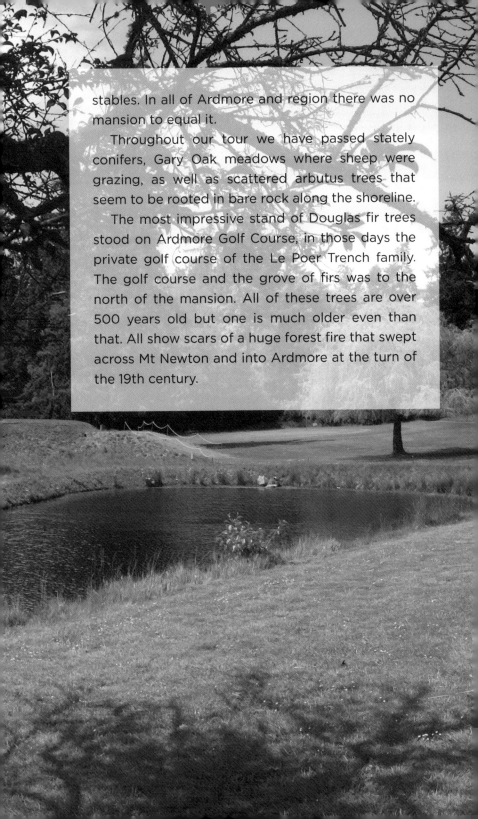

stables. In all of Ardmore and region there was no mansion to equal it.

Throughout our tour we have passed stately conifers, Gary Oak meadows where sheep were grazing, as well as scattered arbutus trees that seem to be rooted in bare rock along the shoreline.

The most impressive stand of Douglas fir trees stood on Ardmore Golf Course, in those days the private golf course of the Le Poer Trench family. The golf course and the grove of firs was to the north of the mansion. All of these trees are over 500 years old but one is much older even than that. All show scars of a huge forest fire that swept across Mt Newton and into Ardmore at the turn of the 19th century.

Sparrow Heaven at Ardmore

Chapter Four:

Story Tree

Before I continue this story of Ardmore, I want to visit that most stately tree. Some have doubted that a Douglas fir can survive to be over a thousand years old. For that reason I invited the British Columbia Forest Service to do an assessment. The foresters did a core drill of the tree and counted the growth rings. The tree was dated as being 1100 years old in 1979. This is not a record since another tree in Washington State has been proven to be older.

The oldest Douglas Fir on record in the U.S. was 30 miles east of Mount Vernon It was more than 1,400 years old when cut, according to McArdle, Richard E., Walter H. Meyer, and Donald Bruce. 1961. "The yield of Douglas-fir in the Pacific Northwest."U.S. Department of Agriculture, Technical Bulletin 201. Washington, DC. 74 p.

The story of the early geology, the occupation of the territory by First Nations, and the surrey ride of 1891, has given some context concerning the beginnings and olden times of Ardmore, but this great tree can give us a different perspective. Reginald Davis, one of the venerable members of Ardmore Golf Course, wrote about the story tree.

Story Tree

In the year of 875, on the Saanich Peninsula, a tiny Fir seedling broke through the fertile soil, inhaled its first breath of pure air, felt the soft breezes and the warmth of the sun upon its tender leaves, then proceeded on an incredible journey through time. Six hundred and seventeen years later, as Christopher Columbus first stepped onto the shores of this continent, this tree, or Th-Kuat, as it was known to the First Nations, stood tall and proud over its domain. Generations of first Canadians had been born and died during these growing years, many of whom had often sought shelter beneath its protective arms during violent storms and oppressive heat. Upon leaving its shelter they would thank the Spirit of the tree for its haven and then continue their nomadic wanderings. Three hundred more years passed. Captain Vancouver came, named the land after himself, charted the waters and rugged coast line, and then left. The tree grew taller and sturdier. Its roots groped ever deeper in its insatiable thirst for water and minerals. Its' leaves reached skyward for carbon and oxygen that it craved, and each year one more ring formed within its' bowels. Three more generations of First Nations were born and died as the tree continued its journey. Fifty more years passed, until Sir James Douglas set foot in Victoria. The tree that was named after him continued to grow unimpressed. One hundred and thirty years later, the tree, now 1100 years of age, 110 feet tall, its girth protected by six inches of gnarled weather beaten bark, its sides still bearing the scars of some past forest fire, is still with us. Massive arms have grown weary and fallen, but the tree still stands magnificent, pensive in its awesome size.

What events it must have sensed in its lifetime. Did it experience Halleys' comet? Could it have felt the pull of the moon? Did northern lights streak across its' sky? Did it feel rays from the Milky Way? Who gave birth beneath its' limbs? Did it listen to the sounds of the land spoken in SENĆOŦEN?

Long after you and I, our children and their children are dead and buried, will it still be growing ? Hundreds of people drive by every day, unseeing, or even aware of this marvel of nature so close to them. Dozens more slice, hook, and curse away beneath its huge size and silent shadows, for it is now the guardian of the third tee on Ardmore golf course in North Saanich. Stand at its feet and look up into its face. Admire its strong body and out-stretched arms towering above you. Marvel at its tenacity of 1100 years, and its survival of both man's and nature's ravages. For those of you who look at such wonders mate-rially, try to estimate the billions of gallons of water it has consumed in its life time, or the board feet of lumber, and number of homes its body could produce, and its value in cold cash. If you are like me you will touch its aged body almost with reverence. You will envy it for its long life, and for what it has seen in silence and storm. Perhaps then you will realize, as I did with quite some humiliation, just how puny and insignificant in comparison we all are.

The Big Tree

du Temple *and* Ostachowicz

Chapter Five:

Land Speculation

Ardmore was a beautiful part of the territory of the First Nations. Having acquired possession of it by means of the Douglas Treaties, signed nation to nation, the settlers via the HBC started to acquire land for homes and farms. At first the Hudson Bay Company's land policies were very restrictive, and large tracts of land reserved for its own use discouraged settlement. The HBC established a joint stock company, the Puget Sound Agricultural Company registered in London. The PSAC agreed to implement colonial land policies that would replicate British institutions on Vancouver Island. PSAC required that a bailiff manage the farms who as in the old country would assume the role of a country squire. The bailiffs were of the 'gentlemen class' and would earn a share of the farm's profit. The workers would be 'indentured servants' who signed a five-year contract to work the farms.

In the 1850s four farms were established: Viewfield, Constance Cove, Colwood and Craigflower. As time advanced, the restrictive land policies of the HBC fell by the wayside and gentlemen established other farms on the Saanich Peninsula. Later on Captain William Le Poer Trench bought the whole of Ardmore for his estate. The drafting of the royal charter of 1849, which created the Colony of Vancouver Island had effectively signaled the end of the HBC monopoly.

Settlement in Victoria and Ardmore was dramatically effected by Britain's declaration of war against Russia in

1854. While most military attention was directed to the Black Sea and the Crimea, the Royal Navy's Pacific Fleet prepared to engage the enemy in the North Pacific by attacking the Russian fortifications at Petropavlosk on the Kamchatka Peninsula. Governor James Douglas promised to provide coal, sheep and vegetables from the farms, and to take immediate steps for the erection of decent and comfortable buildings to serve as a naval hospital. The clinic buildings erected on the Esquimalt Naval Station were called 'The Crimea Huts'.

The Russians repulsed the first assault on Petropavlosk by seven hundred British marines. The Russians wounded or killed one third of the attackers. Since Victoria was not yet prepared for the wounded, the ships after a short stay in Victoria continued to San Francisco. The second attack was anticlimactic since the Russians had deserted Petropavlosk. On returning to Victoria only one sailor required treatment in the newly constructed clinic.

The effect of the navy's presence on the little settlement was enormous. Not only did the navy provide a market for colonial goods, but it also had a huge impact on society. Young officers and sailors stationed at Esquimalt met young women who had come to Victoria in "brides' ships". These ships had brought single women to Victoria to find a new life with bachelor farmers and HBC employees. Suddenly, as well as the locals, the young women had a chance to marry members of the Royal Navy. Many officers decided to stay in the region and asked to be decommissioned or retired. The Le Poer Trench family that would take ownership of Ardmore arrived here because of the operations of the Royal Navy in the Pacific. The colony grew steadily as a retirement location for the British Military and even between 1860 and 1900 was promoted as having one of the most favourable of climates with good land and excellent opportunities..

Between 1900 and 1914 speculation fever reached a state of uncontrolled excitement. Concessions had been granted to the CPR to establish Victoria as a destination port on the Pacific. This minimized the problem of the city's island location. The CPR's "Empress" fleet of sleek ocean liners linked Victoria with ports across the Pacific. The CPR made Victoria a stop over place for civil servants on their way home to England from India, Singapore, Borneo, Hong Kong and other outposts of Empire. The CPR, itself involved in the land speculation, spent lavishly on a worldwide publicity campaign to bring settlers to Victoria. The City of Victoria coined the phrase "Follow The Birds To Victoria" and used the phrase "A Most delightful Outpost of Empire". It promoted Victoria as "a little bit of old England".

In the first decades of the twentieth century land speculators were already scheming to make fortunes.

In 1919, a real-estate brochure published by The Thos. R. Cussack Presses of Victoria described Ardmore in glowing praises. "Ardmore," it reads, "is a beautiful tract of land consisting of 630 acres lying on the west side of the Saanich Peninsula, partly on and just above Cole Bay. This property comprises two of the oldest estates, the Le Poer Trench and the Breed Farms on Vancouver Island. Of the two original farms practically one-half has been for many years under a state of the highest cultivation, for dairying, grain growing, root crops and fruit. The balance of the land is wooded; magnificent specimens of oak, maple, fir, pine, arbutus and some cedar are generously scattered throughout this wooded portion; to tree lovers, prizes that are worth as much as the land.

It would be hard indeed if not impossible to select a more suitable spot for the purpose for which Ardmore has been chosen, your new home for retirement. Ardmore is choice land in every respect, a veritable garden spot, which neither photographs nor word pictures can adequately describe.

The shoreline of Cole Bay and the Saanich Inlet forms the western boundary of Ardmore. Across the Inlet, on the western side is a range of high hills over which runs the famous Malahat Drive. The Saanich Inlet is a long landlocked arm of the sea indented by many attractive bays.

For many years the Saanich Inlet has been the rendezvous of sportsmen: each season seeing the erection of more camps and summer houses in the vicinity of its shores and the subdividing of adjoining acreage into smaller estates to meet these demands.

Saanich Inlet and Ardmore

This beautiful sheet of water, sheltered by the surrounding hills has every appearance of a large lake, and enjoys the distinction of being the largest body of salt water in British Columbia, in which net fishing is prohibited.

Since the waters of the Inlet are protected from the colder winds of the Straits, sea bathing is not the least of its attractions.

Its broad park-like stretches dotted here and there with stately trees, its open meadow land and blossoming orchards, its groves of young balsam and fir, or its sheltered shoreline indented with little bays overhung with arbutus that dip almost to the water's edge, permit of a variety of small holdings that cannot be equaled and certainly not excelled anywhere."

The Great War ended the first real estate boom in Ardmore and Victoria. The next one began in the 1920s

All of Ardmore was once either cultivated farmland or woodlands with a few homes for the farmers, and cabins for the workers. Both the east Ardmore farm and the west Ardmore farm were cultivated extensively. The west farm once extended right down to Cole Bay where sheep grazed and were watered where Cole Bay Regional Park is today. The properties bordering the park were fields for lambing. All that now that has been replaced by housing. The Ardmore Golf Course preserves part of it. A large part of the east Ardmore farm has been replaced by Glen Meadows Golf and Country Club. The remainder of it is the impressive Pendray Farm that now includes the old Frank Edlington Farm.

Fall Colours on Fourth Fairway

Ardmore in 2012 is completely settled. Any further development would require subdivision of the holdings to less than one acre. That would destroy both the remaining stands of trees and the beauty and tranquility of its environment. Blessed by two golf courses and the pristine shores of its fjord, Ardmore will hopefully remain, as it is, a place for genteel retirement in homes that average in price more than those in Oak Bay.

The Ardmore community has played a leading role within the municipality of North Saanich in the development of parks, beach access paths and rural trails. Ardmore residents have been most prominent in developing an Official Community Plan for the Municipality of North Saanich that endeavours among other laudable objectives: to retain the present rural, agricultural and marine character of the community: to protect and where possible restore the natural environment.

Chapter Six:

The First Ardmore Golf Course Built in 1886

In the year 1885, Captain William LePoer Trench purchased a huge property in North Saanich, land that stretched from Coles Bay almost to Union Bay, now Patricia Bay. He named the area, Ardmore. This was in the same year as the completion of the Canadian Pacific Railroad and the 'driving of the last spike' at Craigellachie, 45 kilometres west of Revelstoke.

It was a year for celebration because Canada was now united by steel and locomotive. The government of Canada had just quelled the Louise Riel Rebellion and Chief Pound Maker was on trial for treason in Winnipeg. The building of the railway had taken a toll on human life so high that it should have been a time for sadness and regret too. However, the deaths and injuries of Chinese workers were not recorded because their lives were considered as of no consequence. No one knows exactly how many men died while building the transcontinental railway. Some sources state that three or four Chinese died for every kilometer of track finished.

In 1886, when Lord William LePoer Trench was expanding his estate in North Saanich workers would soon be plentiful. The winter of 1885-86 took a particularly heavy toll on the unemployed Chinese workers with nothing to do, and no money since the completion of the railway. Although most Canadians hoped the laid-off Chinese labourers would go home, some employers along the

Fraser River, in Vancouver, and Victoria were happy to get low cost labour for their construction projects. The so-called China towns that had grown during the gold rush days of 1850s and 60s in Vancouver and Victoria swelled in size and a small one in Sidney became established. The Chinese men became the main labour force for the sawmill and cannery.

Captain Le Poer Trench hired a foreman and a small group of unemployed Chinese workers. They continued the construction of a manor house, livery and stables, plus outbuildings to serve the following facilities; lawn tennis courts, lawn bowling greens, crocket lawns, a cricket pitch, a firearms target practice area, and a nine hole golf course. Some of the Chinese workers lived in a cabin behind the present number eight tee, collected rocks, trundled soil, and dug by hand the water well near number eight green. That well still produces much water for irrigation. It is an excellent well but two Chinese workers lost their lives while digging it.

Milton Towers, who lived in the gatehouse after the burning of the mansion, recounted the following history. Lord William Le Poer Trench ordered the construction of the Ardmore well. Four Chinese men worked on the project, two would take turns digging and passing up buckets of blue clay, while the other two carried the clay and piled it. As they dug deeper they used pulleys and ropes to haul the loads to the surface. They dug deep to about 40 feet. They shored up the walls of the well shaft as they descended using skills learned while working on the completion of the transcontinental CPR. They finally hit a giant dome of rock that prevented further digging. They observed very little water, only a slight seepage coming into the otherwise dry well shaft.

The Lord of Ardmore was not impressed. He ordered the men to use their railway learned blasting skills. They would set explosives and demolish the rock, remove the cracked remnants and continue to dig until he had his water. They set the dynamite and ignited the charge. When the smoke and debris settled they could see the rock was now cracked and that water was bubbling up into the shaft. The Lord ordered that the Chinese descend immediately into the well to repair and shore up the shaft. While two of the four were down in the bottom the lower part of the shored up shaft collapsed. The men were crushed and then drowned. William Le Poer Trench decided to leave the bodies of the Chinese entombed at the Ardmore well since the water was only to be used for agriculture. This is a scandal of Ardmore that is little known. However, this was a time when Chinese were hardly considered people in British Columbia. Between 1891 and 1926, 33 Chinese victims of the leprosy were sent to D'Arcy Island to die, slowly, painfully and without the benefit of even basic medical attention. In Eastern Canada, white people with leprosy were cared for by Catholic nuns, a resident doctor, and provided with excellent accommodation and care. Chinese people with the disease were transported to D'Arcy Island close to Sidney, B.C. No nurses went there, no doctors set foot on the island, and the ill had to live in dreadful shacks. Their only contact with the outside world was a supply ship that came every three months to drop off food, clothing, opium and coffins. Medical and Sanitary officers on these ships reported that conditions were deplorable, yet for years nothing was done. Chinese people so dreaded the lazaretto on 'Arcy Island that many committed suicide before they could be imprisoned there.

"Island of Shadows" a film distributed by FILMWEST ASSOCIATES is highly recommended as a resource historical film. The writer also recommends the book, "A Measure of Value, the story of the D'Arcy Island Leper Colony" by Chris Yorath.

The Le Poer Trench family had come to North Saanich by sea. They had not come overland from eastern Canada, neither had most of the residents. They had been lured to Vancouver Island by advertisements in prominent Imperial newspapers. The island was a haven for people from the British Isles, British India, and the tropical colonies. People from the frozen interior of North America were in a minority. Historian J.F. Bosher writes that not enough attention is given in historical accounts to the maritime, and imperial nature of early settlement on Vancouver Island.

An attempt had been made to settle Vancouver Island by means of a policy entitled 'systematic colonization' advocated by the planner, Edward Gibbon Wakefield. The policy sought to reproduce in Victoria a British class structure of society with a density of population that would lead to the propagation of the arts and good manners. A landed class with substantial holdings would import the required number, the ideal percentage, of tradesmen, farm workers, professionals, Anglican ministers and so forth such that a little England would be recreated. The policy failed because new comers would not stay close to Victoria when so much good land was available for the taking .However, for many decades, people commented that Victoria looked and felt British. Even the policemen wore bobby hats, a high hard helmet.

Captain Le Poer Trench built his mansion, supported the Anglican Holy Trinity Church in Patricia Bay, and made his choices of sporting activities for his estate that befitted a lord and fulfilled most of the Imperial expectations of Wakefield. Le Poer Trench helped Holy Trinity acquire its first organ, and was a benefactor of the arts.

Priscilla Jay wrote the following on March 20th 1985 in an issue of the local weekly newspaper called 'The Review' in those days.

" ...The Ardmore Farm was split into an east farm and a west farm, either side of the West Road. For several years the east farm was owned by R.H. Breeds who built a house on the crossroad near the intersection with the West Road. He was a hop grower and a building containing the kiln was demolished in the 1940s.

The West farm became the property of Captain and Mrs. William LePoer Trench. He was a son of the Irish Earl of Conardon. They established an Irish demesne in North Saanich.

There was a gatehouse on the West Road and stone pillars either side of a winding driveway through tall fir trees that led to a mansion overlooking Cole Bay. The area surrounding the mansion was terraced and at the lower levels were tennis courts, golf course, and aviary."

An article in the Peninsula News Review of May 18th 1949 reports the following:

The article has the caption, "Two Stone Pillars Still Stand Guard".

"On the West Saanich Road, close to the sea, stand two huge stone gate posts. They stand as a monument to yesterday. Time was when through those gates lovely ladies in crinoline and lace, British officials and leaders of Vancouver Islands' cultural life made their way to partake of the festivities at Manor House.

In Cole Bay British warships were always happy to drop anchor and officers to go ashore as guests of the Le Poer Trench's.

The Le Poer Trench's, living on what is now the Ardmore estate, knew how to entertain. Suddenly it all ended. It ended one night in a blaze which glowed for miles around.

What caused it? There are several stories told by old-time Saanich pioneers but the most commonly accepted one is that the lord of the mansion understood Europeans better than Indians and once in a fit of rage shot an Indian's dog.

The next night the house of a million memories was ashes. All that remained were the gatekeepers' house and two stone gates which today still keep their lonely vigil. They lean just slightly forward as if listening for the ghostly coach wheels and gay voices which echoing on a summer night will proclaim, Manor House has come back into its own again."

As a young lad I walked through the charred granite foundations of Manor House and stood between the leaning gates. Mr. Milton Towers, who lived in the gatekeepers' house, hired me as a teenager at hay cutting time. As we paused in our work he would sometimes tell me more stories and theories about what caused the demise of Manor House.

He told me that the Lord had not just shot one Indian dog. He had shot several. The fire had started suddenly on a windy night against the southwest wall. Servants had discovered a pitchfork missing from the livery stable and a trail of wispy hay leading to the place where the fire ignited. While the Lord was sleeping somebody had taken huge pitchforks of hay, thrown the hay against the wooden wall just above the granite foundations, had ignited it and fled. The pitchfork was found close by.

The Lord immediately blamed the people in the Salish Paquachin village at Cole Bay who would have had a clear view of the blaze. But Milton Towers said that the Lord was a so called 'ladies man' a sort of Casanova known for sexual encounters with prominent women in Victoria, and even with the Chinese servant girls. We will never know for sure who burned the Lord out of Ardmore. But it is wrong to just suspect the Salish. Servants, or relatives of girls sexually mistreated, or a dispute between lovers could have led to a retaliation. The only thing we can know for certain is that the burning was no accident.

Never has a Lord so suddenly fled the scene of his own mansion burning. Within a few months the Lord had sold the Ardmore Golf Course and Estate, and had returned to Ireland. His sudden departure was proof to many old timers that the Lord was in fear for his own life.

It is amazing that a nine-hole golf course, the Ardmore Golf Course, had been built in 1886, five years before this journey by surrey. Only a private desire for playing the 'royal and ancient' game of golf, and the wealth to afford the construction of a lordly estate, had made that a possibility in this pioneer district.

Transportation from North Saanich to Victoria and reverse for social and sporting events at Ardmore required time and planning. The early transportation choices were horse and buggy, stagecoach or the railway. The roads were made of packed earth and became almost impassable in the winter. For that reason the Victoria and Sidney railway in operation between 1892 and 1919 was the preferred method of local commuter transportation.

Julius Brethour of North Saanich was the main intiator of the service. The old steam engine burnt nothing but cordwood, always stopping once or twice en route to fill up with water from a large wooden tank and also to restock wood from piles left adjacent to the track. The train, know affectionately as "The Cordwood Limited" was reported as being self-opinionated and would loiter at frequent stops. The carriages even then were ancient relics of a long-past, grand service on a first-class railway, but the plush-covered seats were dirty. The railway was not dependable. In fact there were many letters of complaint.

The first letter of complaint was published on November 2, 1895, in the *Province* newspaper of Victoria by a disgruntled passenger who signed his letter as W. M. Le P.T., the one and the same William Le Poer Trench. He complained that because the train was three hours behind schedule he had arrived late for a theatrical presentation. Shortly afterwards Le Poer Trench purchased the first Stanley Steamer on Vancouver Island.

Le Poer Trench liked to hold receptions at his manor for the elite of Victoria. Golf could be played at Ardmore Golf Course, tennis or lawn bowling enjoyed on a sunny afternoon. But transportation was always a problem.

The British Columbia Electric Company began operating an electric interurban tram service in 1912 between Victoria and Deep Cove. This provided better and more reliable transportation service to Ardmore. However, by that time the Le Poer Trench family had returned to Ireland.

One can say with historical accuracy that Ardmore Golf Course has been non-continuously in the same location since 1886, the year after the Louise Riel Rebellion of 1885, a record of some significance in terms of the early days of golf in Canada since the Victoria Golf Club and course was not established until 1893.

William LePoer Trench had introduced golf as a sport in North Saanich. Citizens of Victoria and officers of the Royal navy, who had come to social functions as invited guests, and had been impressed with the challenges of the game, decided to build a course at Macaulay Point, Esquimalt in 1891.

Men from the Royal Navy began by clearing four holes in order to practice the royal and ancient pastime. Lieutenants George Barnes and Frederick Templer, of the

Royal Artillery and both golf enthusiasts, put their men to work to complete nine holes. There were two par threes, six par fours and one five hundred yard long, par five dog leg. Nearly all of the holes afforded excellent views of Juan de Fuca Strait and the Olympic Mountains. The course became known as the United Service Club.

Former Attorney General, Harry Pooley, in the Daily Province of November 13, 1943, mentioned the next reported construction of a golf course. He states that a golf course was laid out at Beacon Hill in 1889. From the LePoer Trench private Ardmore Golf Course, golf had moved south, to Esquimalt, then Beacon Hill and finally to Oak Bay in 1893 with the establishment of the Victoria Golf Club.

Because the Victoria Golf Club was the first club that built a course and became properly organized with a constitution and Board of Directors, and to hold official club competitions and club championships, it is recognized as the oldest golf club on Vancouver Island. However, history proves that William Le Poer Trench built the first golf course on Vancouver Island at Ardmore.

Chapter Seven:

The North Saanich Golf Course Built in 1907

After the tragic burning of the Le Poer Trench mansion in 1904 Ardmore Golf Course became an orchard and once again part of Ardmore Farm. However, golf having been introduced to Vancouver Island in North Saanich it appeared again in about 1907. North Saanich residents who had witnessed and experienced golf on the Ardmore Estate now formed what they named the 'North Saanich Golf Club'. It was located adjacent to the Tseycum First Nation's community in Patricia Bay immediately to the north.

The North Saanich course consisted of nine holes. Par for the course was 31. There were four par four holes and five par three holes.

When the club returned to the location of the Le Poer Trench Ardmore Course 15 to 20 pages of history was removed from the front of the original ledger to start with a fresh slate. According to a footnote in the margin of the ledger (put there by Mr. White) the pages were removed from the course and sent to somewhere in the RCAF for safekeeping. Unfortunately they have been lost so the exact facts are not clear. The date of 1907 noted in the margin of one of the first pages indicates that the North Saanich course operated from 1907 or earlier.

Details from the "Daily Colonist" dated May 23, 1926, prove that the course was located off West Saanich Road opposite Downey Road, on the old Mallowmot farm. It

was a little over 2000 yards in length with natural undu-
lating features plus large oak and birch trees providing
natural hazards.

On December 7th 1927, the first constitution and bylaws
were written. Signatories were Constancy L. Layered of
Deep Cove; John Law & J.J. White of Sidney; Charles Birch
& Guy Pinwake of Patricia Bay; and Wilfred Sisson, the
secretary & manager.

On March 22nd, 1981, Priscilla Jay interviewed Mrs. Elsie
Sisson. The following is part of that audio recording from
the Provincial Archives that is here transcribed.

Priscilla Jay gives a brief introduction to the recording
as follows:

*"Mrs. Sisson and her husband, Wilfrid, came to North
Saanich in 1920 and for a few years enjoyed a life of
"leisure and pleasure". When financial circumstances made
this impossible, they started breeding Chinchilla rabbits. It
is not known if they were the first breeders in this area,
but since they were able to sell most of their stock for
breeding purposes for several years, they must have been
early in the field. When this market was reduced and it
was necessary to sell pelts, they found the work distaste-
ful, and Mr. Sisson became associated with Mr. Singleton-
Wise at the North Saanich Golf Club, which was located
north of the Pat Bay Indian Reserve on the West Saanich
Road. When this land was no longer available, the Sissons
rented 50 acres from the Ardmore Farm where they built
the Ardmore Golf Course which is now owned by the Du
Temple family."*

The voice of Mrs. Elsie Sisson:

*"For relaxation, my husband played golf at a little course
in North Saanich which was started by Mr. Singleton-Wise
of Deep Cove and called the North Saanich Golf Course.
One day Mr. Singleton-Wise told Wilfrid that he was sorry*

to have to tell him that he would be closing the course at the end of the season as he was losing money on it. He had to pay high rent. At that time it was $50.00 per month. He had built a house on the premises, part of which was a clubhouse and the rest a residence for the man who did the work. As it happened, the rabbit business had become very humdrum. Everyone who wanted Chinchilla rabbits as an investment was satisfied and we no longer could get a market for our two does and buck. It was down to the nasty job of killing and skinning and selling the pelts. Wilfred was ready for a change. He asked Mr. Singleton-Wise if he could keep the course going if instead of hiring someone whom he had to pay $30.00 a month, we did the work for free in exchange for living in the house. There would be two of us to look after the green fees: I would be in the house to collect the green fees while he would be doing the work on the course. There was no mowing of the fairways to do because Mrs. Rider of Mallowmot Farm ran her flock of sheep on the place. Mallowmot Farm extended from the Horth Cross Road to the West Road and the Indian Reserve. The course was a small block of only fifteen to twenty acres. It was a short course but quite tricky and they had sand greens. Mt. Singleton-Wise thought it would be an excellent idea.

I think the two men had a very loose arrangement.... If you can make anything out of it they agreed to share the profits. We were there several years from 1929 (1929 – 1933) and got a little club going. It was a very friendly club. It was a great social club for the ladies. They didn't take their golf seriously. No handicaps or Ladies' Golf Union. But finally we could not get the rent renewed at a price that we could pay so the men looked around for another site. And that is when the Ardmore Golf Club was formed in 1933."

Greens keepers constructed a fence around the sand greens to keep the sheep from walking on them. Motor oil was added to the sand to increase the surface tension. After the players had putted out, one of the golfers would pull a sisal mat around the green in circles from the centre to remove footprints and to level the surface.

Sand Greens sketch by Zena Rogak

Chapter Eight:

The Resurrection Of The First Ardmore Golf Course in 1931

Wilfrid Sisson and golfers from North Saanich resurrected, redesigned and rebuilt the Ardmore Golf Course of Le Poer Trench. They leased it from Arthur E. Haynes, agents for the new owner, Allan Steam Ships Ltd. Work on the new course started in 1931 and would be completed two years later. It would be a community effort of everyday folk, farmers, and retired military officers.

The plan to move golf back to Ardmore occurred in 1930 when rents were increased at the Pat Bay site. This also happens to be the year when Bobby Jones won the U.S. Amateur crown for the Grand Slam of golf at Ardmore, Pa., on September 27 at the Marion Golf Club that was established in 1896.

Average golfers had talked about the unlikelihood of anyone actually accomplishing the grand slam emblematic of victory in the British open, British amateur, American open and American amateur championships all in one year. But journalistic speculation had grown, and interest had peeked. Then suddenly Bobby had done that convincingly to become the greatest golfer of the time. In fact no one has accomplished the grand slam since. He had won his fifth American amateur championship, and his thirteenth major championship.

Golfers in North Saanich, young and old, must have been invigorated and inspired as they started to prepare the fairways, greens, bunkers, and tee off locations at the former golfing layout of William LePoer Trench in Ardmore. Bobby Jones had raised greater interest in golf among sporting people by becoming an amateur golfing legend. For one moment in time golfers could feel some consolation during the stock market crisis of the 1930s.

Golf had not been on the radar in North Saanich before this upsurge in interest created by events far away. Tennis, lawn bowling, crocket, horse back riding and archery had been more popular as sports than golf. These were sports known well to the retired officers and gentlemen of the British Empire who had settled for retirement in Victoria.

Alan Steamships Ltd of Scotland owned large parcels of land in Ardmore stretching from Cole Bay to Patricia Bay. At that time the land was still being used for growing hay, corn and potatoes and apples. Having now moved to this new location the name was changed from the 'North Saanich Golf Club' to the 'Ardmore Golf Club' to correspond to the original name given it by Captain William LePoer Trench.

Golfers in Bird Habitat

Mr. W. T. Sisson, Mr. Pat Hope, and Mr. Birch cooperated in designing the course layout and planning the community effort to build what would become The Ardmore Golf Course and Club. Mr. W. T. Sisson suggested that narrow fairways be crafted between the crop fields. All the work was to be accomplished by volunteer work parties. Sand was purchased from a local supplier and placed in nine locations for the greens. The Course at Ardmore opened on April 19, 1933 for play on seven holes. The official opening ceremony occurred on June 7th 1933 for play on nine holes. One hundred and twenty-five golfers attended the opening ceremony.

The original 'hole cups' were made from one-pound jam tins. The ladies had made flags from the cloth of 'Roses Flour' bags and sewed the numbers 1 to 9 onto them. The sand greens would be replaced by grass greens in 1934. The diameter of the grass greens was no more than five meters. The sand from the old greens was deposited to the left side of the first fairway and placed around a mound made from rocks picked from the fairways and greens. The kidney shaped sand bunker on the left side of number one fairway is the oldest and first sand trap on Ardmore.

Mr. Sisson was the manager of the property for the landowners and was also the first secretary of the golf club at the new site. It was his responsibility to oversee the property for Alan Steam Ships Company of Scotland and to manage the funds of the golf club.

Messrs. Hope and Birch were the first executive members on record. It was through their hard work and dedication that the Ardmore Golf Club presently exists.

In the beginning the 'Ardmore Golf Club' rented the Ardmore Estate property from the landowners. The club owned and managed all the golfing operations. The manager, Mr. Sissons, wore two hats. He managed the property for the owners and worked for the golf club. He managed and worked the hay and vegetable production. He maintained and made changes to the course, paid the rent to the property owners, and managed the club's monies. He was paid a yearly salary, and sat on the golf club board of directors as the secretary treasurer. Mr. Sisson held the position for 15 years until the property was sold to new owners.

This new beginning was a time of hope and a time of difficulty. Citizens wanted to learn golf and to emulate Bobby Jones but then the 'Great Depression' took a greater hold and there were many trying times at the Ardmore Golf Course. Membership dropped and fewer people were playing golf. The new club had rent to pay and fewer funds were coming in. It was a constant battle to continue. Nearly every year rent payments were negotiated with the property owners to lower the rent. However, even with lower rent the club continued to go further into debt. *(Note: The outstanding debt was finally paid off in 1937. At that time all members were assessed a $2.00 levy to pay off the debt.)*

Even during these trying times, the members were not thwarted. They continued to improve and modify the course. While hay was still harvested and sold to local farmers the hay fields became narrower as the fairways were widened. Changes were made and the course was maintained thanks to the volunteer work done by the members. Among the many alterations was the installation of new sand traps. Three hundred feet of water pipes were installed to No.1 green, white pegs were placed along the road on the west side of No.4 fairway to indicate 'Out of Bounds', and several alterations were made to hole Nos. 5, 6, &7. Present day golfers owe thanks to these early members for their hard work, dedication, and conviction to make the golf course a viable resource for future generations.

In an audio recording at the B.C. Archives Mrs. Elsie Sisson reports:

"We hand sand greens for several years but we were always thinking of the time when we could have grass greens. Unlike the old North Saanich Course we did not have sheep to keep the fairways down – and sheep make a course very dirty and unpleasant and that was a thing that Wilfrid was adamant about. He would not cope with that again. He purchased a mowing machine – a horse drawn one. The ground was too wet to have a tractor on it until we got a lot of tile draining done. So we used to hire an old white horse from the nearby Indian Reserve. The place was very stony. The members got together at one time and had a stoning bee. Everyone was asked to bring a pale and a tool, if possible, and we made a big party of it.

We decided the time had come to have grass greens. At the general meeting it was decided to raise the dues to $12.50 a year, and to raise some debentures – at $10.00 for each debenture. And listen to this: any member getting a debenture would need to pay only $10.00 a year. Thus he would get $2.50 a year as interest and repayment. At the end of four years he would be fully paid back."

Mrs. Elsie Sisson says in a B.C. Archival audio recording the following about buying a tractor:

"Oh, I didn't tell you about when we got rid of the horse driven mowing machine and acquired a tractor. The horse was a very slow form of mowing, and there was a lot of work to do. The club's very good and generous friend, Mr. Guy Pownall, donated his old Model T Ford and we had it converted into a lightweight tractor, which pulled a five-section mower. "

It was also used for watering the new grass greens that were cut by a newly purchased push mower.

Original 'Membership Fees' were set at $10.00 per year, and there was no entrance fee. A family membership was $18.00 per year. At that time there were not many green fee players, however, these fees were 50 cents per day or 25 cents for nine holes.

Note: To become a member: A prospective member had to be accepted by the membership before they could join the club. The prospective member had to be sponsored by a member in good standing. They had to post his/her intent to join, on the bulletin board (in the prescribed area) for a minimum one-month period. Then a meeting would be called and the membership would vote on whether or not to accept the hopeful prospective applicant.

The Golf Club was set up consisting of the Parent Division, the Ladies Division, and the Men's Division. The Parent Division was the head of the organization and held the Constitution. The Ladies Division was run under the hat of the Parent Division. However, they ran their own competitions and managed their own monies. The Men's Division was run and managed under the Parent Division, including all finances and competitions.

The Ladies Division of the Ardmore Golf Club became members of the C.L.G.U. in 1932. They were one of the first nine-hole golf courses in British Columbia to become members of that organization. They continue to be members to this day.

The Parent / Men's Division became members in the Royal Canadian Golf Association for the first time in 1937. This membership was dropped in 1939 and was not picked up again until several years later.

Chapter Nine:

Ardmore Golf Course and Ardmore Golf Club

The war years were most difficult. Many of the members had enlisted and had been sent overseas to fight in the war. The Ardmore Golf Club continued to operate even through difficult times mostly because of the woman of the local families. On the other hand Augusta National in Georgia, perhaps because it was a male only club, despite many attempts to keep the club open during World War II, was forced to close in October of 1942. To make money, the Augusta members used the land to raise cattle and turkey. Toward the end of 1943 Augusta housed over 200 cattle and 1,400 turkeys. The turkeys turned a profit, but with a ceiling on the price of turkey, the high cost of beef, and the cost of repairing the course after the animals grazing made the project a make-even at best endeavor. The course reopened again on Dec 23, 1944.

Ardmore remained open throughout the war but some concessions had to be made. In order to increase hay production the club manager made the fairways narrower. Three additional mowers were purchased. One was a new hay cutting sickle bar to be pulled by the modified model T ford tractor. Both the original hay cutter and hay rake have been on display behind the present second green on the walk from #5 green to the #6 tee. Hay was still grown and harvested for dairy jersey cows. New cups were purchased for the competitions, and a new sign was erected near the airport. One improvement of note was the lengthening of the eighth hole (present day fourth hole) in 1941. The area was plowed and seeded by members at a cost of $25.00.

This was also a very busy and interesting time at the club. Although many changes to the normal daily operations were necessitated, some new endeavors were taken on with great vigor and anticipation. The following paragraphs indicate just some of them.

In 1940 the club passed a resolution to have a junior program. The age limit was set at 18 years or younger. Juniors, other than those from family members, were subject to a $5.00 annual fee.

From 1940 to 1943 competitions were altered due to the fact that membership was at an all time low and monies were not available. The Parent Division reduced the number of competitions to be played. Initially, the ladies club cancelled the Thursday club functions, then finally in 1943, it was decided to stop all championship competitions for the duration of the war except for the J. J. White trophy competition that continued.

In 1941, members of the CLGU across Canada were raising funds to help in the purchase of a spitfire aircraft, to help the war cause. Special 'Spitfire Days' were held during which donations were collected. The Ardmore ladies dug deep and made a substantial donation towards the endeavor. They are mentioned in the history of golf in British Columbia, 'Backspin' by Arv Olson, as having raised three times their allotment per capita. This was the best in the province of B.C.

Both the men and the women contributed to the Red Cross and sent knitted clothing and bedding articles to Britain, and socks and cigarettes to the fighting forces.

The golf course premises were offered to the Ardmore Rescue Personnel for their use in the case of an emergency.

George Du Temple First Landing at Pat Bay Air Station

In October 1939 an event occurred which would eventually change North Saanich, Sidney and Ardmore Golf Club. Wing Commander George Walter du Temple, on instructions from the R.C.A.F., landed a biplane Avro Tutor Model 626, Biplane Trainer, Serial #225 in a field owned by the Jones family near the site of the present terminal building of the Victoria International Airport.

On October 13, 1999 the Peninsula News Review published an article entitled, "History in Making".

"October 22

1430 hours – took off from Vancouver Airport

1511 hours – landed at the Victoria airport. Condition of runway is good... weather cloudy.

October 23...raining heavily. Arrangements made with local businessmen for necessary supplies – milk, butter, eggs, beef, etc.

18- man squadron installed at Jones House

October 24 – establishing a hangar (in what was the Jones family's barn)

Officers set up the Collier house...

The year was 1939, and the airmen writing the journal was George Walter Du Temple, leader of Squadron 111 and pilot of Avro 626, the first military plane ever to land at what is now the Victoria International Airport. His co-pilot was Corporal Rusty Hopper.

The air base was established after War was declared and because Ottawa was concerned that the British Columbia capital city had no protection from air invasion.

On the ground, Du Temple and Hopper set about their preparations. They arranged for the original 14 airmen to be quartered in the Jones house, and for their transportation they arranged a Model T#360.

George Du Temple had one duty that brought him great pleasure and a measure of pride. He hoisted the first windsock at the airfield – a windsock made by his wife Alice...."

G. W. Du Temple had orders to oversee the construction of a military airfield. Thirty airmen from Squadron 111 came by steamship to Victoria and then to Sidney. Landing strips were to be prepared with farm tractors and rented graders. The landing strip was graded down railway bed that headed the aircraft up through a cut in a stand of very tall trees toward the seaplane base. The planes took off east or west depending on wind direction.

Ardmore, and North Saanich / Sidney experienced the noise of air defence for the first time. The whole of Squadron 111 moved from Sea Island to Pat Bay bringing four Lysanders, that enabled the squadron to patrol the coastline. A variety of planes took off over Ardmore roaring the afternoon and disturbing the silence of the greens. The RCAF occupied the western side of the field. Their aircraft included a DH Gypsy Moth, an Avro 626 Tutor, Westland Lysanders MK 11, Blackburn Sharks MK 11, Fairey Battle MK1, Fairchild 71 and two Stinson HW 75 aircraft.

The station grew rapidly. The RAF arrived and occupied the eastern side of the field. At first the RAF had Bristol Beauforts, then Hampdens, both torpedo bombers.

In addition to maritime patrols, RCAF aircraft intercepted numerous Japanese fire balloons designed to be carried by the jet-stream at high altitudes and land in the coastal forests to create fires. Coastal B.C., Washington and Oregon received many of these.

Two local eateries that benefited from the building boom at the airport were Mary's Coffee Bar, located at the east end of the airport property and the Blue Moon Café situated on the west side.

Aerial View in 2012

As well as overseeing the construction of the airport as Commanding Officer, Mr. G.W. du Temple and some of his airmen learned to play golf at Ardmore Golf Club. The golf course facilities were made available to members of the R.A.F, the R.C.A.F., the R.A., and the R.N.Z.A.F. stationed at Patricia Bay. The fees set at 50 cents per month from Nov 1st to April 30th, and 75 cents per month from May 1st to October 30th, with clubs supplied. The same Mr. du Temple who negotiated these arrangements would buy the golf course in 1946 after decommissioning from the R.C.A.F.

Golfers also came to Ardmore from the RCAF marine section that grew to the size of a small navy. Both RCAF and RAF personnel were involved. Many types of vessels were used, including bomb dinghies, 38-foot crash boats, larger supply vessels, similar to an 80-foot fish packer and motor launches. Two high speed launches were also employed on rescue work, powered by two Packard Merlin V12 engines. They could disturb a good putt all the way from Cole Bay.

**View of Ardmore in 1946 with The Bamberton
Cement Factory Visible in the Saanich Inlet**

While many military personnel played golf occasionally, they were almost given that privilege as an appreciation of military service. The club could not carry on with its financial requirements including the yearly rental of the land. The owners decided that they wanted to sell the property. The club was approached on May 16th, 1946 and given the opportunity of purchasing the land. After much discussion it was resolved that the club could not obtain sufficient funds among the members for the purchase. As such, the owner made a decision was made to sell the Course to a private buyer.

The year 1946 was both the end of an era and a new beginning. It was a time of loss and a time of gain. Members found it difficult to accept the changes. The members had done the hard work both in building and improving the golf course, and in the erection of club facilities and purchasing and maintaining equipment. They had toiled for many hours doing the maintenance of the fairways and greens. They had fought constantly to keep the course running.

Now the club could not make the necessary payments to the owner despite modest reductions in the rent. All those years of hard work and constant effort might be lost. Now, like it or not, an outsider would own and run the golf course they had constructed. Ardmore had been the private club of Le Poer Trench. Then friends and neighbours had made a community golf course with volunteer work. Would a developer buy it? Would it stay as a golf course? No matter who took over the changes would be hard to take.

On October 31st, 1946, the Ardmore property was sold. Mr. George Walter du Temple purchased it. He had learned of the intended sale of the property earlier in the year and decided to purchase it, as a family venture, with the intent of keeping it as a golf course. However, the rural telephone party lines, which were shared between five to seven homes buzzed with rumors. Many imagined big development ideas. Anyone who had built an airport would probably build a resort. Mrs. Alice du Temple reported in her diary that she was questioned daily far too often but the suspicions did not subside. However, the du Temple family had really decided to continue both the farm and golf course aspect of the property.

George W. du Temple, who had been a General Motors sales manager in Vancouver before enlisting in the R.C.A.F., was made manager of Davis Motors (presently Empress Motors) in Victoria. His intention was to use part of his salary to make payments on the property mortgage and to improve the golf course. However, this meant that work on the farm and golf course would be the responsibility of his wife, children and relatives.

The du Temple family consisted of Mr. and Mrs. du Temple and their three sons. The eldest son was Ronald George du Temple who was 18 years old. The middle son, Barry George du Temple was 9, and Wally George du Temple was the youngest at 6 years. The house they had acquired, the old Sisson home, had 800 square feet of living space, with two bedrooms, living room, kitchen, and washroom. There was a 400 square foot clubroom with washrooms at the western end of the cottage. That old clubroom later became club storage room C. The cottage in 2012 still stands on the walk to the sixth tee, parallel to Ardmore Drive.

Ardmore : Departure and Arrival is the story of how Wally remembers leaving Vancouver and arriving at Ardmore Golf Course in 1946.

"The Photo Portrait of Wing Commander Dad was the last item to be put into the car. I was hugging it. I had

rarely seen my Dad since birth. He had been away at war. Mom had made him real for me by inventing Daddy stories. Occasionally he had parachuted candies and teddy bears into our back yard from the sky. I would carry these to his picture at bedtime Mom leading me.

I first knew Dad as image, black and white photo in a grey uniform under glass or held him as embroidered red wings outlined in gold. Mom lifted me at night to smudge wet lips on the cold glass of his air force face. I knew Dad also as silver steam when late at night by taxi in the rain we waved at a puffing train my image receding from the station.

Taking my seat I hugged the framed picture of my Dad as if he wasn't yet home and driving the car. Loaded under a tarp we trailored china, bedding, clothes, silver ware, a piano, a sofa, an armchair, and an antique chair favoured by the family cocker spaniel. All else had been sold. My first adventure was starting with a steamship ride away from Vancouver to a far away Vancouver's Island.

We arrived at the corner of Ardmore Drive and West Saanich Road in a polished black Packard sedan on the 31st of October 1946, Halloween. The pavement vanished as Dad wheeled the vehicle and trailer onto the muddy ruts of Ardmore Drive. "This isn't a 'Drive',"Mom said. My Dad, George Walter du Temple drove the car. My Mom, Alice Louise du Temple, sat opposite in her fine-feathered hat, her milliners' arrival bonnet. Her silky cocker spaniel, Oddity, sat with her three sons Ron, Barry and Wally in the back seat to protect her society dress and silk stockings.

The move from an upscale Vancouver district had been made necessary after the Dad's decommission from the RCAF as Wing Commander. The General Motors dealership did not return his pre-enlistment job but found another one for him in Victoria. He had chosen home and property without discussion like the commanding officer he was. He knew that the digs to which he was leading his family could not match the mahogany balustrades, hard wood floors and luxurious drapes of a Point Grey two level home. He was probably apprehensive but didn't show it. Alice was obviously nervous because she had been permitted to bring so little from her fine home. Dad said,"Remember Dear, you are going to a rural area. The house will be cozy but smaller. It's a much larger holding with farm animals, meadows and hedgerows. Some neighbors come to play golf between the hay fields and will even pay us for the privilege. It is a good investment."

She knew that Roy and Lilly Walker, her sister and brother-in-law, were included in Dad's big plan. They would be coming to work on this farm that had a golf course playing through it. A portion of the property would be sold to them for their home.

The car sloshed to a stop beside a sagging one-car garage. Close by stood a narrow rectangular building. An inspection began of our new dwelling. Mom guided the cocker spaniel, Oddity, on a new leash.

There was a very small room for sales of golf tickets, farm produce, paraphernalia and confectionaries. There were two bedrooms, a kitchen and a tiny living room heated by a potbelly wood stove. A wood burning oven range would turn the kitchen into a sauna when in use. A tiny bathroom was equipped with toilet, claw foot tub and closet. Two by four stud walls were finished with tongue and groove unpainted wood. Light fixtures were dangling electrical cords with bulbs swinging from sockets. Dad promised again that all of this was temporary because he would build a dream home soon, a promise that was ful-filled a decade later.

Mom returned to the Packard. She wept. She sat there as if she would never get out. Dad encouraged her to show her 'stiff English upper lip'. As a kid I didn't know what that meant but I knew Mom was proud of it. I'd look at her lip and shortly she would assume a stronger posture, push her shoulders back and take several deep breaths. Mom was still a proud Brit who with her family had lived in London through WW1. The unloading proceeded with military precision.

My big brother Ron, eighteen and strong, wondered where young girls could be found. He helped Dad do the unloading. My brother Barry and I, nine and six years, went exploring around the property. Mom made what decisions she could about placement of the chattel.

Mr. and Mrs. Sisson introduced some golfers and neighbours. They had been renting the property from Allen Steamship Company of Scotland from which Dad had made the purchase. Milton Towers and wife owned a two hundred acre sheep farm that occupied all of what is now Glen Meadows Golf Course and extended to Coles Bay. They brought us a gift kitten and some dressed lamb. Mrs. Fraser and her daughters, Diane and Daphne, lived in a two storey, Victorian type mansion to the north. Ron eyed the Fraser girls with a lack of interest. They were shapely black haired beauties but already middle-aged spinsters. In the weeks to follow Ron would use all of his cunning to get Dad to buy him a used Chevy coupe. After all the son of a dealership sales manager should have a good used auto. He was thinking 'dragster'. His speeding, racing and spinning exploits would soon begin.

The Fraser girls invited the family to a welcome dinner. Dad had bought roman candles and other wireworks so later we made a bonfire, set off explosions and rocket launched red, white and blue clusters of falling stars.

After that it was off to bed. I was told to sleep but that was hard. I had a new home, a new kitten, a Mom who was upset and a big brother who resented being forced to move from his friends. As senior child he had been the man of the house until Dad returned. He was muscular, spirited and carried himself cool like James Dean. Both Mom and Ron had grown accustomed to making their own decisions. Dad wanted to make them now. Emotions often jumped like beads of water in an oily frying pan.

I walked bare foot on the sliver dangerous floor to kiss Oddity goodnight. She was my black and white silky Lady and Mom's darling. Kneeling beside her relocated throne I caressed her soft dangling ears. She had a stately chair. Carved teak legs curved upward and swept around a crest shaped back. With an air of 'I'm not pleased ' she sat regally on button-crimped upholstery embroidered with golden leaves. I followed her almond eyes as she critically assessed her new surroundings. She glanced at the dust covered wood crackling pot-belly stove, at the dark tongue and groove walls, at cobwebs and spiders on the ceiling and at the discoloured ivory keys of the piano where the intruder kitten was washing it's wretched bum. Oddity raised her lips and uttered an oath such that the kitten kaboom, kaboomed the keyboard as it jumped and scrambled away beneath the sofa. I named her Scrambles. As Oddity tucked her nose into a cushion I could hear the drip drip of a faulty faucet and then the flush and gush from the toilet followed by a prolonged wheeze as the reservoir refilled. A musty smell came from clay and damp rat scat in the crawl space. The floor timbers were propped up by stones.

After good nights were called out by each of us, I could hear Mom and Dad engaged in a whispering duel they thought was private. Mom had read in the local weekly that the Oscar winning best picture of year "The Best Years of Our Lives" by Samuel Goldyn was showing at Sidney's Gem Theatre. Mom made some sarcastic comments about our future prospects. Sound penetrated all interior and exterior walls. They were empty of insulation." The next day the whole du Temple family needed to start working on a farm that had a golf course playing through it.

The Du Temple family helped organize the first opening day tea party to mark the beginning of competitive golf for the season on May 24th 1947.

Opening Day Tea

One of the earliest events at Ardmore Golf Course was a contest between the best archers in the region against the best golfers. In order to make the contest between the archers and the golfers competitive the archers had to aim at half way targets in order to reach the golf green in regulation according to the rules of golf. Archers shot their finishing arrow at a tennis ball that sat on a bottle.

Barry and Wally were soon trained to milk the jersey cows morning and evening. Another chore was to prepare golf balls for resale. During the war and immediately after new golf balls were in short supply, so Wally and Barry were given the job of continuing Mr. Sisson's golf ball reconditioning workshop. Experienced golf balls found in the hay fields would be cleaned, dried and repainted. Paint was applied by poking a pin into the cover of the golf ball, and then by dipping the ball into a special paint and then spinning the ball on a thread. The balls were then hung from the ceiling on cords for the coating to harden.

While these jobs had a potential to be helpful clearly older workers were needed. The greatest weight fell on the shoulders of the eldest son, Ron du Temple, who already had shown a huge talent as a carpenter and mechanic. Ron would build all of the additions to the home and clubhouse working together with his Dad evenings and weekends. But there was more work than Ron, George and Alice could handle.

In this regard, the du Temples asked the sister of Alice du Temple (Lily Walker, with her husband Roy) to move from Vancouver and to build a home on part of the property and to become the first employees. Several acres were subdivided from the holdings, which in those days extended from West Saanich Road to Heartfell Road and Ardmore Drive. One of their sons, Philip Walker, would also work on the property. Roy Walker was a mechanic by trade and had also run a farm in Manitoba. These were considered to be good qualifications to work on a farm, which had a golf course playing through it.

For many years hay was produced for two jersey cows on the property. The family grew a big variety of vegetables. Free-range chickens had a special territory with houses for protection from raccoons at night. A large aviary produced an abundance of noise and multi-coloured budgies that were sold to pet shops in Victoria, or from the pro-shop.

The du Temples sold eggs, butter, milk, and veggies in excess of what was consumed by the family. All of these items were in the Pro Shop along with golf balls, tees and clubs.

Mrs. Alice du Temple was proud of her butter production because of an innovation she had made to her oscillating washing machine. This was the type that had rollers at the top for squeezing water out of the washed laundry. She had asked Ron to make an insert that would slip down over the fins of the gyrator. This was a circular piece of plywood with a hole in the centre, and three slots for the fins. He added buckles and straps on each slot to hold the sealer jars. The thickest of the jersey cream was skimmed from the milk production and put into the jars. Alice would strap the cream filled bottles in place and start the washing machine. After about fifteen minutes she would remove the butter and form it into shape. She sold the blocks of butter in the pro shop. She liked to show her invention to golfers who doubted that she had made the butter in her washing machine.

The Du Temple Family Home and Pro Shop 1950

Once the course was privately owned there were new changes to how things had been run. The club would no longer manage or maintain the course. However, members of the club gave advice to help the new owners.

Sometimes members would want to do things their own way, and came into conflict with the new ownership. One example concerned the purchase of the first gasoline greens mower. It was much heavier than the push lawn mower. It had steel rollers and many more cutting blades. The members considered this to be too heavy and would compact the greens. Mr. du Temple was annoyed by the opposition but strategically agreed to continue with the present push mower were members to donate their time to push the mower. Silence descended on the meeting and Mr. du Temple bought the new mower.

The club no longer functioned as a business, and as such, the membership now became recognized solely as a club under the B.C. Societies Act, and remains that way today. The club, from that day forward, became known as the Ardmore Golf Club, playing from the Ardmore Golf Course. The club sold all equipment and assets, excluding trophies, to Mr. du Temple for a sum of $538.61.

As a new organization the club was required to make some changes. The existing club funds were tallied and distributed. The club had retained a total of $200.00. The balance was paid to Mr. Sisson in recognition of his many years of service to the club. The president, vice-president, and secretary were granted authority to sign cheques for the Ardmore Golf Club.

The du Temple family members were given memberships in the golf club. Mr. du Temple would pay a grant to the club in the sum of 5% of the entrance fees and yearly dues paid to him by the members of the club. Mr. du Temple sat on the board of directors as the secretary treasurer, for the first few years.

Ardmore Golf Club and Ardmore Golf Course Ltd., became two separate organizations. While their histories are intertwined each has a story of interest in the history of Ardmore and North Saanich..

Mr. du Temple operated the golf course as a business. He continued to make improvements to the course in the late nineteen forties. He enlarged the greens, and aerated and top-dressed them. He then applied herbicides as necessary. He installed a tiled ditch at the left corner of the sixth fairway (now No. two fairway) that widened the fairway. Family staffers posted winter and general rules at the first tee.

The Walkers and du Temples constructed and leveled wooden box tees. The business bought new rubber mats made from old car tires and installed them to replace the old sisal mats. They would build grass tees much later.

The young du Temples hand watered the greens by gravity feed. The old ford Model-T tractor had three (45 gallon) steel barrels that were attached behind the front seat. One of these barrels sat upright in the middle with the others lying sideways to either side. The only water source on the property was the dug well on fairway number eight where the gazebo is located, the one dug by the Chinese workers hired by Le Poer Trench. A one-cylinder Massey Ferguson motor with pump was situated there. It was the type that had a huge flywheel that one cranked with one's whole body before the motor would start. Family members would start the motor, and fill the three forty-five gallon drums. Next one would start the Model-T often times also by cranking since the electric start was faulty. One would deliver the water to a green, and then, by holding a hose slosh the water directly onto the turf. Golfers could seek relief from puddles on the greens.

In the early years the pins on the greens were quite different than what we have today. The typical hole consisted of a large fruit can inserted into the ground, the pin was a steel rod approximately five to six feet long protruding from the hole, and the flag was a white flour sack fashioned and sewn together to allow it to be hung from the steel rod, with numbers sewn onto it. Mr. du Temple changed the holes and the flag to the recognized PGA regulated hole size and substituted the flour sacks with proper flags. Reducing the size of the holecups did not help Mr. du Temple to win any popularity contest.

From the time when the course first opened there were no course starters at the club. Using a ball selector rack located at the first hole did the method of determining player selection off the first tee. It consisted of two chutes in which to put your ball. One side was marked as 'No.1' and the other as 'No.10'. When you wanted to tee off you put your ball into the rack in the appropriate chute, where it gradually fell to the bottom. When your ball came out at the bottom it was your turn to tee off. The ball rack was set up so that balls would drop alternately from each shoot to ensure players continuing from No.9, to play the back nine, would

Dragon Fly Pond at Ardmore

alternate with those just starting to play. This ball selector rack, although not fool proof, had relied somewhat on the discretion and honesty of the players, remained in use until the early 80's when a Pro Shop Starter was designated to announce the tee off times for golfers.

Left to Right Alice Du Temple, George Du Temple, and Betty Bradley who would marry their son, Ron Du Temple

The Model T was both the tractor and watering system for the golf course. Ron Du Temple at work 1947.

Chapter Ten:

Injury and Death in the du Temple Family

1950 was a year of near tragedy for the du Temple family. Ronald du Temple, the son of Mr. and Mrs. G.W. du Temple had just celebrated his 22nd birthday on August 18th. Then on August 20th while on vacation Ron dove into Okanagan Lake from a float that was anchored by cement blocks. He hit one of the blocks and floated to the surface face down with a broken neck. He drowned but was revived thanks to the professional first response of Penticton Volunteer Fire Department.

The prognosis by the attending Doctor Stapleton was that Ron had a fifty-fifty chance to survive without severe brain damage and paralysis since his spinal cord was partly severed. Fortunately, Ron recovered completely during the next few years.

In the days after the accident, the entire du Temple family, including Elizabeth (Betty) Bradley travelled to Penticton to be with Ron at the Penticton hospital. Ron and Betty became a married couple in 1952.

The club members stepped forward as a community to support the du Temple family in this time of crisis and to assist them in keeping the course functioning with the guidance of the Roy and Lillian Walker family. This was the North Saanich and Ardmore neighbourhood working together in a heartfelt way.

**Wedding Day of Ron and
Betty (Bradley) Du Temple**

Nobody had constructed a separate practice area therefore the du Temples designated certain fairways and greens as practice areas. Management posted the hours of practice to avoid regular playing times and banned practice on weekends. They required that members pick up their own golf balls promptly.

In the late 1950s Percy and Rae Criddle had made an offer to buy Ardmore Golf Course from the George Walter du Temple. Mr. du Temple took some time to consider the offer but decided not to sell. The Criddle family had the idea of making Ardmore into an eighteen-hole course.

The Criddle family owned a nine-hole golf course, several tennis courts and a cricket pitch on a 5000-acre farm in Manitoba, south of Brandon. They had built the facility themselves. After much soul searching they had decided to sell out and come to Vancouver Island. All family members had agreed including the senior Criddles, Stuart, Maida and Evelyn.

Grandma Sadie du Temple stands between her son, George Walter Du Temple, and her grandson, Wally Du Temple on the ninth green

When buying and expanding Ardmore was no longer an option, Mr. Percy Criddle purchased a 140-acre parcel bordered by McTavish Road and West Saanich Road and began making an eighteen-hole golf course in 1961.

George Walter du Temple held the belief that a both a nine-hole and an eighteen-hole golf course could co-exist in Ardmore and that the market for each was different. In time his analysis proved to be correct.

While building Glen Meadows the elders of the Percy Criddle family joined Ardmore Golf Course and completed in the club competitions. Glen Meadows opened for business in 1965. It is rare for a golf course to be family owned. Here were two families, and two golf courses privately owned. They have co-operated both as businesses and families for the betterment of golf on the Peninsula.

In 1961 Mr. and Mrs. du Temple had planned a vacation to Tahiti. Mr. George Walter du Temple had been born in Tahiti and educated in New Zealand, and had not been home since coming to Canada in 1919. He had intended on finally introducing his wife Alice to his relatives in Papeete and Auckland but died of a massive coronary heart attack one week before the anticipated departure. At this time both Barry and Wally du Temple were out of province following their teaching careers, having both graduated from U.B.C.

Ron and Betty du Temple who were prepared to manage the golf course during the planned trip were now faced with managing the golf course for the widowed Alice du Temple not just for a few months but full time as an occupation. Alice du Temple went into a depression that lasted for many years. This was a difficult time for the family of Ron and Betty du Temple. The house was very small for a family of six - Ron, Betty, Cindy, Penny, Brad, Rhonda, soon to be eight with the birth of George and Theresa (Teri).

Under these circumstances, Ron and Betty simply took charge and did an excellent job. They continued to improve the golfing experience for players at Ardmore.

From left to right, front row: Teri, George and Rhonda, back row: Penny, Cindy and Brad

Betty du Temple reorganized the Pro Shop and expanded the variety of golfing products that were offered for sale. Betty also expanded and improved 'tea and sandwich service' which Alice du Temple had started. Betty's home baking, with fresh home made bread and sweet cinnamon buns, and fresh roasted coffee all from her kitchen became very popular. Tables were set up on the lawn in front of the cottage. The old flagpole station near club storage room C was where Betty would serve her goodies.

Betty was a take-charge person and became an excellent entrepreneur. She also took an active role in the ladies competitions and became an excellent player.

Ron Du Temple, along with Barry and Wally were given an equal number of equity shares when Alice Du Temple had the company Ardmore Golf Course Ltd., incorporated on March 29th, 1962. She kept all three voting shares in order to keep control of the company.

Ron du Temple built a new workshop for the golf course machinery, expanded the pro shop, added some sand traps, and built the first reservoir for an expanded irrigation system. At this time all sprinklers had to be installed by hand at night. Valves with couplers were installed to sprinkle the aprons and approaches to greens. The old hoses that were nightly pulled onto the greens in sequence remained. A worker went out nightly between 11pm and 3am during the driest parts of the summer. No irrigation of tees was necessary since all the tees were still on rubber mats. The fairways had no irrigation and browned off in the summer.

Ron ended all hay operations. He bought a three blade rotary mower-tractor for the rough. Staff now maintained the former hay fields as second cut rough. A new gang mower and tractor were purchased for the fairways and a Toro greens mower for the greens. The golf course was no longer partly farm.

The influence of Betty and Ron is still everywhere to be seen. Betty planted the giant California Red Wood (Sequoia) that stands near the third green. Betty and Ron purchased the seed for this tree in California during a holiday. They nurtured the tree in the kitchen that Ron built and then transplanted it to where you can see it thriving today. Ronald George du Temple passed away, a victim of cancer, in 1973, the tenth of December on his Mom's birthday.

Wally and Barry du Temple left the teaching profession in 1972. They would manage Ardmore Golf Course together until Barry decided to accept a principalship of an elementary school in Quesnel. Newly married to Olga Valentova, Wally would soon have two children, Evan du Temple in 1973, and Hana du Temple in 1974.

Left to Right Hana du Temple, Jaroslava (Mother of Olga), Wally, Olga and Evan du Temple

In 1973 members and golf course staff rushed to the assistance of Mrs. G. W. du Temple whose home, behind number six green, 814 Ardmore Drive, had burst into flames. The house was totally consumed by fire and smoke such that entry to the dwelling was impossible. The North Saanich Voluntary Fire Department arrived promptly, and discovered that Mrs. du Temple's car was not in the garage. Fortunately, Alice du Temple was in Sidney doing some shopping at the time.

Mrs. Alice du Temple, and her son, Mr. Barry du Temple, who had been boarding at his mothers' home, moved into the Ardmore Cottage to live with Wally du Temple, his wife and small family.

In the seventies the course stopped paying the annual dues for the CGLU and RCGA fees. Because of increasing competition for market share in the golf industry the management had decided to encourage more green fee play and to schedule office tournaments on weekends.

There were many changes and alterations made to the course during these years. Wally du Temple planned and made these changes happen. The existing lower water pond was increased by nearly four times the original area and deepened to forty feet for a massive increase in volume. This was built in the area between the present ninth-hole fairway and the dogs-leg seventh-hole fairway.

Olga du Temple, a retired surveyor, helped to plan the shape and heights of the berms. Wally's wife for many years would maintain these embankments free of yellow gorse.

This area had been used for potato growing and hay production. Wally installed an automated computer controlled sprinkler system to allow for volume controlled watering of the fairways, greens and grass tees. He had recently built grass tees to replace the rubber mats. This project was vast in scope and required the borrowing of a large sum from the TD bank. From construction of the huge reservoir to the newest of irrigation technologies, professional contractors did the planning and installation at the request of management. A fence was installed around the base of the huge reservoir and donkeys were purchased to graze the slopes.

The property was becoming all golf course with top quality manicured fairways, greens and grass tees and automated irrigation. On the other hand, although the fairways had been made wider and the turf was becoming excellent, one could not ignore the donkeys, horse and mule that roamed the off fairway roughs.

As a part of community outreach Ardmore Golf Course had established a Donkey 4-H Club. The donkeys mowed the grass on the walls of the reservoir and rough areas during the day, and stayed in the barn a night. The barn was built between the third and fourth fairways. A riding ring was built to the south of the barn where the practice pitching area is today. Stalls were rented out by the golf course to several parents.

Mr. Ron Evans built a donkey golf cart with a love seat and bag holders for two newly weds. This golf cart was rented out to staff party tournaments, weddings and stag parties with a driver. The cart was the first and the last of its kind on the island. It now contains flowers near the entrance to the golf course lounge.

Golfers regularly brought apples and carrots in their golf bags to feed the donkeys. The sound of seven donkeys 'heehawing' and dashing to the pasture fence in anticipation of a treat was part of the rural ambience.

Golfers out for golf in a donkey golf cab

In later years a golfer complained of being pushed and overturned by Thumper the mule while looking for a golf ball. The lady in question had been bending over to look in the clumpy pasture grass when Thumper the mule put his muzzle between her legs from behind and lifted her abruptly for a head over heels spin. Legal action was threatened. Then a lady fell while climbing over one of the stiles that permitted entrance up and over the pasture fence. Her court case was successful and damages were paid. After that happened the pasture compounds were removed. The animals in the future would remain in the reservoir area that was behind a fence and out of bounds. The pastures became second cut rough once again except for the area between No.1 and No.2 fairways that became a protected Garry Oak meadow.

The golf donkey cart rental came to an end. Brides and grooms, or office managers would now have to walk or rent a gas golf car. Issues of safety and liability concerns put an end to the unique donkey golf carts.

Ardmore Golf Course saved the lives of several mis-treated donkeys and gave them refuge. The Mustard Seed

Street Church volunteers led by Gipp Forster and Peter Plunkett-Norris saved the life of Neighdeen, a standard grey donkey. That was the start of a donkey sanctuary at Ardmore Golf Course. The Donkey 4-H Club took a leading role. Moreover, Ardmore Golf Course actively supported the Mustard Street Food Bank and set up a collection system in Ardmore with the golf course as the deposit depot.

The donkeys annually led the Christmas pageant in Victoria with Neighdeen carrying Holy Mary while other donkeys stood in the nativity stable and ate hay from mangers beside a ceramic representation of Holy Jesus. Parents and children of the donkey 4-H learned how to feed and care for the animals. They learned how to harness and to show the donkeys at the Saanichton Fair. The children either led the donkeys or drove the donkeys in the Sidney and Victoria Day parades. They even started the first Santa Claus Parade in Sidney, the first and only entry in 1981.

Baby Randy Checking Out Golf Shoes At The Clubhouse

The Donkey 4-H Club used every opportunity to advertise the Ardmore Golf Course as its' sponsor with signs,

The Second Green Guarded
By Gary Oak Trees

floats and trophies. The float pulled by the donkeys had a sign on it that said, "The Better Business Burro recommends Ardmore Golf Course". After many years of public viewing 'The Victoria Better Business Bureau' threatened to sue for defamation. Wally responded that the Ardmore burro always did better business and that defecation was a natural right of donkeys. Moreover in parades the kids used shovels and buckets to clean the streets.

Alice du Temple was a great supporter of the donkey sanctuary at Ardmore. She was distressed by the ill conditions that many of donkeys suffered before being referred to Ardmore. Wally and Olga needed years to correct over grown and hooked hooves among other maladies. She authorized the construction of the donkey barn that is situated between the third and fourth fairways.

In 1980, Wally du Temple changed the sequence of the holes played by renumbering them. He made fairway number six into the present fairway number two. He renumbered each hole after that so that hole number nine became hole number five. He then built a long trail past the Pro Shop to the renumbered hole number six. He made the change in order to bring the golfers back to the clubhouse after the fifth hole. This would permit golfers to use the washrooms in the clubhouse after half of their nine-hole game. It would also give golfers an opportunity to purchase a snack.

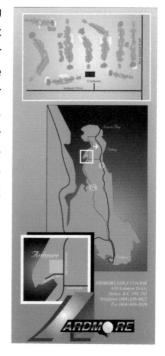

Chapter Eleven:

The Trees of Ardmore Golf Course

Since 1946 the Du Temple family has planted trees on the Ardmore Golf Course. Many of the older trees predate the arrival of both the Le Poer Trench and Du Temple families. The Le Poer Trench family planted five varieties of apple tree including the 'Charles Ross' apple, a handsome, juicy and versatile English classic good for old fashioned cooking. Golfers can also pick two varieties of Japanese plums, 'early golden' and 'santa rosa'. The variety of trees on the property is immense. Here is a partial listing: Gary Oak, Douglas Fir, Western Red Cedar, California Redwood, Rocky Mountain Juniper, Lodge Pole Pine, Western White Pine, Grand Fir, Western Hemlock, Maple, Weeping Willow, Tuliptree, Pacific Madrona, Eastern Cottonwood, Paper Birch, Western Yew, Pacific Dogwood, Hawthorn, Pacific

Can You Spot The Eagle's Nest?

Crab Apple, Choke Cherry, Red Alder, Acacia Trees and Quaking Aspen.

When golfing enjoy the trees and birds. Perhaps bring a field guide to help with identification. Our forefathers were on intimate terms with the trees around them and understood the glory of how they function: the roots holding the tree in the ground, absorbing water; the leaves creating food for the tree out of water,light and air, and giving off oxygen in the process; the trunk supporting the branches and holding - right under the waterproof protec-tive bark - all the tubes that take water and minerals up to the leaves and then food down from them.

Ardmore Features A Beautiful Variety of Trees

Chapter Twelve

Open Tournaments

In 1978 the golf course management initiated the first ever Ardmore golf tournament. It was known as the 'Ardmore Thanksgiving Classic', and was, of course played in October. The tournament was open to all golfers, both men and women, throughout the district. The tournament was organized with two separate divisions of competitions, one for the men and one for the ladies. Each division had its own set of prizes and trophies. The tournament ran for four years, the last one being run in 1983.

In 1986 Mr. W. du Temple, the course manager, approached the Parent Division to take over the tournament. He proposed that the word 'Thanksgiving' be removed from the name. The Club would incur the work required to make all arrangements, including advertising, acquiring and organizing prizes, tee times, etc. However all monies brought in, including all the green fees, and other profits made during the tournament would go directly to the 'Golf Club'. A vote was taken and it was carried that the men's division would accept Mr. du Temple's offer. The new tournament was to commence on October 3rd, 1987. However, this did not happen. The tournament was not resumed until 2009 as a fund raiser for ALS and the David Pendray Memorial Endowment Fund.

The Bill Smith Pro-Am

The trophies for the Ardmore Thanksgiving Amateur Classic were used for a period of six years as a birthday Pro-AM for the beloved Ardmore golfer, Bill Smith. One pro and one amateur played as teams in a best ball format. From his 99th birthday to his 105th birthday the team of Bill Smith and Harry White was victorious. Bill passed away just prior to the tournament for his 106th birthday. Bill Smith was recognized with a world record for the oldest player to ever win a sanctioned Pro-Am Golf Tournament. He was 105 years old for the record.

Home Of The Ardmore Thanksgiving

GOLF CLASSIC

PATRONIZE OUR SIDNEY MERCHANTS APPRECIATED HERE FOR ANNUAL SUPPORT.

SIDNEY RADIO SHACK
HARVEYS SPORTING
GOODS
SIDNEY HARDWARE
SIDNEY MUSIC
ALEXANDER CANE
MENS WEAR
TOWN SQUARE SHOES
CHRISTINE LAURANT
JEWELLERS

CHAMPION

ISLAND FURNITURE
SIDNEY GLASS
SIDNEY GIFT SHOP
FLINT MOTORS
BEACON TRAVEL
JUS RITE PHOTOS
CORNISHS BOOK AND
STATIONERY
SLEGG LUMBER LTD.
CLOVERDALE PAINT
AND PAPER

Wally and Barry Du Temple at the start of the Ardmore Thanksgiving Golf Classic in 1978.

Chapter Thirteen:

Fairway Number Five Redesigned

In 1986, Wally du Temple altered the course layout for reasons of public safety. Fairway number five used to play parallel to Ardmore Drive from an elevated tee at the corner of Ardmore and West Saanich. The green for the hole occupied part of the present parking lot. Ever since the hurricane of October 12 and 13, 1962 when winds with gusts to 145k had blown down an ancient Douglas fir that had stood between Ardmore Drive and the golf fairway, golfers had often struck errant shots onto Ardmore Drive.

Without that huge fir tree golf balls too often hit cars, and several pedestrians complained of near misses. Wally du Temple finally decided to redesign the hole before a tragedy occurred. He decided to build a new green for hole two that would be guarded by two Gary Oak trees.

**The Old Ninth Green. The Douglas
Fir That Blew Down Can Be Seen
on the edge of Ardmore Drive**

du Temple *and* Ostachowicz

Green number two would become the green number five. He turned the direction of tee number five away from Ardmore Drive. Golfers would now aim their golf shots through an arch of branches formed by the massive fir trees. The Du Temples thought about the community when

At Ardmore you are treated like a member of the family. We know that exercise can be fun in a friendly and inviting atmosphere. We also offer exciting excursions for your entertainment and relaxation.

The tee for fairway #5 or #9 was at the corner of Ardmore Drive and West Saanich Rd., and played parallel to Ardmore Drive to a green near the parking lot

they redesigned the fifth fairway. Ardmore Golf Course has played an important role in many community projects.

Ardmore Golf Course helped the local communities of Sidney and North Saanich to build the Mary Winspear Centre. Ardmore Golf Course promised to donate five thousand dollars per year for four years for a total of $20,000.00 and challenged other businesses to do the same or more. Wally du Temple was among the most active members in the fund raising committee that was masterfully led by Mr. Richard Holmes.

In addition, Ardmore Golf Course sponsored four chairs in the Charlie White Theatre for the cost of $2,000.00 each. Betty and Wally purchased these chairs and installed name plaques in memory of Alice Du Temple, George Walter Du Temple, Ronald Du Temple and Barry Du Temple.

Two children had crept underneath the roots of a huge Douglas Fir where rot had made a sort of cave. Their camp fire could have brought an end to the ancient grove had not the The Sidney Volunteer Fire Department responded with full force. While firefighters doused the flames that ran skyward Ron Du Temple and the Hartshorn brothers used chain saws to fell the tree while it was still burning. That was the only way to stop the tree-fire from crowning.

Chapter Fourteen

The Course Between 1980 and 2010

In 1980's the clubhouse was extended and a new office and reception area were constructed. The addition was built out from the north end of the existing building.

Alison Lee, who had been hired by Barry du Temple, continued as the golf course manager for a record of sixteen years of excellent service.

In 1989, an arborist confirmed that a giant Douglas fir tree near the fifth hole was unsafe. Management made the difficult decision to cut a magnificent tree for safety reasons. The fir had tipped over slightly toward the south after a heavy gale. The roots appeared to be lifting the soil. To make something better out of a bad situation, Olga du Temple suggested that the stump be left very high and that a cougar be carved and placed on top. Mr. Gordon Langston, a local wood carver, used his chain saw to carve the body of a cougar from a large block of cedar. Employees used a crane to lift the sculpture of the cougar onto the stump. The cougar stands on the top of a thirty-foot trunk and is a landmark for all to enjoy as motorists turn onto Ardmore Drive from West Saanich Rd.

Betty (du Temple) Snobelen passed away on the 29th of July, 2008. The members and the du Temple family held a celebration of life at the clubhouse. The family concluded the celebration of life and memorial with a procession up the fourth fairway to the California Red Wood that Betty had nurtured in her kitchen and then transplanted. Fairways number two and three were temporarily closed as the entire fleet of electric golf carts made the journey and together with all the people circled around that tree in meditation.

The Cougar Sculpture

After the passing of Betty a new management board of Ardmore Golf Course Ltd., was formed: Wally du Temple, Cindy du Temple and one person designated as the representative of Rhonda, Brad, Terry, Penny, Cindy and George, the sons and daughters of Ron and Betty du Temple. George du Temple was elected.

Mr. Greg de Jong was recognized and thanked for twelve years of outstanding service as Superintendent of Grounds Management. Greg de Jong is the first quali- fied golf superintendent that Ardmore has employed. Mr. Greg de Jong, made many improvements to Ardmore Golf Course between 1990 and 2011. He leveled number two tee and shaped it into a platform of two decks. He leveled the front of number six green to create an extra pin placement and improve drainage. He installed a continuous gravel path to connect all nine holes so that motorized golf cars can be used year round. He created a designated practice area with a sand bunker for short game improvement. Next he built a golf teaching area with an open grass tee, covered mats and a retractable net. Greg rebuilt the number six tee so that the red markers could be at 251 yards for a par four. The white markers would be for each hole played as a par three. He placed red markers to indicate the front nine, and white markers to indicate the back nine on all tees. In order to give some separation and protection for the expanded number six tee, he built a small pond and placed a wire mesh fence on its southern end. Next he realigned the ninth fairway to accommodate the new sixth tee. The tee at the pro shop was realigned to create power cart parking. He rebuilt tee number four into one with two decks and added a garden for enhancement. He rebuilt tee number seven and leveled it.

Golfers Enjoy Birdies at Ardmore

Greg lengthened hole number eight by building a back deck for a distance of 151 yards. Next he rebuilt tee number nine into a platform of two decks. He moved and reshaped the bunkers in front of green number nine.

He added new fairway bunkers to fairways number three, four and nine, and built a greenside bunker at green number two.

He set out a five year plan to install drainage on previously wet fairways. While this is an ongoing project most of the plan has been completed. To create additional features and interest in play he added mounding between fairways number one and nine. He planned and supervised the enlargement of the middle reservoir to catch winter run off for irrigation. Excavated material from the expanded pond became the elevated tee for an alternate number seventeen, back nine tee off. The distance would be 95 yards over water. For winter play, Greg built an alternate grass tee at fairway number three.

Superintendant Greg de Jong has been applying the latest best practices for the environmental stewardship of the property. The golf course website features a slideshow program entitled, "Birds Over Ardmore". These photos and the associated bird count indicate that birds are thriving on an environmentally friendly terrain. Deer, raccoons, river otter, and muskrats, field mice, salamanders, and frogs together with the birds use Ardmore as a refuge and home.

Please enjoy a few of the photos taken on Ardmore Golf Course by the amazing photographer Don Delaney.

Greg de Jong created the Gary Oak Meadow between fairways #1 and #2. It is an Environmentally Sensitive Area. It features a natural nursery for baby Gary Oaks, and Camas, Chocolate Lilies and heritage grasses. This is an 'out of bounds' area for golfers. Students from 'environmental science' at the University of Victoria participated in the restoration project.

Chapter Fifteen:
Birds of Ardmore Golf Course

Don Delaney has been an avid birder since the age of four when his mother gave him his first bird picture books and took him on nature walks.

He has been carving birds since 1990, and for the past six years bird photography has been a passion. His photos have won awards at the Reflections of Nature Show in Saskatoon and for the past two years at The Atlanta Audubon Society Annual Photo Competition.

For two years and for several seasons Don Delaney photographed birds in Ardmore, and on Ardmore Golf Course. Only a small selection of bird photos can be featured here. The complete catalogue of 'The Birds of Ardmore' can be viewed at the Ardmore Golf Course website: http://www.ardmoregolfcourse.com/ See: History.

Don's complete collection of bird and carving images can be viewed at: www.flickr.com/photos/donaldsducks

Chickadee

California Quail

Hooded Merganser male

Hooded Merganser female

Golden-crowned Kinglet

Ruby-crowned Kinglet

Fox Sparrow

House Finch female

House Finch male

Ringed-neck Duck pair

Red-winged
Blackbird male

Red-winged
Blackbird female

Canada Goose goslings

Crossbill male

Downy Woodpecker male

Pileated Woodpecker male

Mourning Dove

Wilson's Warbler

Cooper's Hawk

Northern Flicker

Chapter Sixteen:

Ardmore Golf Club Between 1950 and 2010

Our artificial pond that covers three acres now looks and feels very natural and is the home to muskrats and a family of river otters. Raccoons, geese, ducks and eagles are often seen at this location. Deer frequent the pond and slopes early each morning. While cougars appear here only on rare occasions sightings have occurred.

In the 1950s the Club established a more stable position. The membership had grown and the club had a bank balance of $319.64

The ladies saw the revival of several competitions. They included the Ladder Matches, Spring Cup (A, B, & C levels) and the Spoon Competition, spring and Fall Eclectics, the Championship Cup, J.J. White Cup, Metal Auto Sales Cup, and the Field Day. All once again were to be competed for. A new event, the 'Sweepstake Competition' was introduced. The Parent Club gave replica trophies to members winning any cup for three consecutive years.

In the decade of the 1950's a great number of changes happened to the club. The club membership averaged 111 members. The club was strong financially. Rules were passed on how to maintain the funds, and in 1950 a motion was passed to ensure that the bank balance of funds never be reduced to less than $200.00. Mr. du Temple discontinued his grant to the club. This created some concern to the membership. Therefore a motion was passed the following year wherein each member will be assessed a $1.00 annual fee to cover club expenses. This fee was to be collected by Mr. du Temple at the time of membership dues, and was to be turned over by him, to the secretary treasurer at quarterly intervals, as received.

Some of the existing competitions were altered in the way they were played and a number of new cups and competitions were added to the fixture lists. In 1950 the ladies changed the Eclectic Cup to the 'Par Cup' to be played throughout the season. Winners of each bi-monthly Par competition would qualify to play for the cup at the end of the season. Mrs. Gamble donates a new 'Auto Sales Cup'. A new Ring (Eclectic) Competition commences; it is to be played every two months from May to October.

In 1950 Mrs. Gwynne initiated the twilight foursome competitions. The intent was to create an evening of fun and competition between the men and ladies of the Club. It was initially started and managed by the ladies division. Later the parent club managed the event. The competition occurred twice a month in July and August. It began as an 11-hole competition. Start time was at 6:30 p.m.. Partners were drawn, with teams consisting of one man and one woman, to play in two-ball foursomes. In 1951 a cup match was added. This was to be played for on August 27th. In 1953 it was changed to every Thursday at 6:30 p.m., from June 18th to July 31st. In 1955 the twilight foursomes were extended to begin in May. The club charged each person 25 cents to pay for prizes. Prizes were distributed to the 'first' and 'second' place winners, and if warranted by number of players, to the 'third' place winners.

In 1951 the club added two new cups to the ladies fixture list. Mrs. Taylor donated the 'The Button Challenge Cup'; and Mr. Rose donated the 'Margaret Rose Cup' in memory of his wife.

Members donated many trophies for tournament play. Mr. Frank Green and Mr. G.L. Hay donated the 'Perpetual Button Trophy'in 1955. In 1958 Captain Barr donated the 'Barr Cup'. In 1959, Mr. and Mrs. G. du Temple donated the 'Bronze Button and Trophy'in; Captain and Mrs. Barr donated the 'Ball and Chain Barr Cup'; and Mr. A. H. Donald donated the 'Donald Trophy'.

Both club divisions made changes with regard to the rules of play. For instance, the Spring Cup that had previously been played as a one-day, 36-hole competition was changed into to two 18-hole rounds on two consecutive weeks.

The club gave out of district members full voting privileges. The membership approval committee decided to post the names of prospective members on the notice board, on a Club Application Form, for a two-week period. The committee declared that if there were no objections made by existing members, that the applicant automatically would become a member. This policy was discontinued for membership in the 90's.

In 1956 for the first time, the General Meeting and Annual banquet was held away from the club facilities at a new location, that being in the private dining room of the Sidney Hotel.

In 1958 the Constitution and Bylaws were rewritten to replace the original written in 1927. Many of the old bylaws were outdated and did not reflect the requirements at that time.

The 60's continued to be good, busy times for the club. The membership had grown from approximately 120 members to 185 members in 1969. Attendance at the Annual meetings and dinner continued to grow, increasing from 40 members to 90 members toward the end of the decade. The men joined the RCGA for the first time and also joined the Regional Golf Association. The RGA, now known as the "Victoria & District Golf Association", organized and managed interclub competitions. During these years some of the existing Ardmore Club Competitions were revised in the manor of play, and/or new schedules are devised. There are several new competitions and trophies for the parent, men's and ladies divisions of the club.

1960 was the year that a junior committee was formed to help assist the junior members. A new cup, the "Handicap Championship Cup", was donated to the men's division by Mr. Arthur Steward. The first winner is Mr. Sutherland. The ladies extend the Eclectic Matches from three to four to be played from April 1st to October 14th.

The president and vice-president both resigned from their positions. With no one stepping forward as replacements, Mr. du Temple agreed to act as president for the remainder of the year.

In 1961 the field day competitions, which were always played in the daytime, was changed to evening play, to be played for in early July. Mr. W. du Temple makes a complete list of cups and trophies for information purposes.

A vote was taken and passed that for the very first time permitted juniors to play in the 'Twilight Foursomes'. To qualify they had to provide a score card signed by an adult member showing a score of 65 or less for 9 holes. (*Note: This motion was again brought up in 1967 and was again passed with the same provisions as above.*) The ladies added the rule that the junior must be at least 16 years of age.

In 1962, the membership grew by 35 members to 178. The men joined the RCGA and the RGA. Mr. du Temple was tasked to take an extra $1.00 from each male member to pay for the RCGA entry fee, and $1.00 from each lady

Pond On Left Side of Ninth Fairway

to pay the CLGA fees. Joining the association brings with it some new rules and regulations. A new handicap system must be conformed with, wherein, a player must have a minimum of 25 games to make up their initial handicap, and all scores must be recorded. In competitions, any playing member without an established handicap will be regarded as a scratch golfer. It also inspired added interest in the junior golf program. The Ardmore club hosted a one-day seminar and lessons, given by professional golfer Mr. Richard Munn.

The rules for the ladies "Button Challenges" changed. To arrive at a handicap to be used for this competition, both the challengers and button holders added their two handicaps together. They then divided the total by two and take ¾ of the average dropping any half strokes.

In 1963 the ladies button matches were extended to run a full year, from October 1st to September 30th of the following year. Silver Rose Bowl was purchased for nine-hole Parr competitions. New to the schedule, a nine-hole round robin competition was started. The competition was to be played for over the winter months, from November to May.

In 1964 the du Temple family donated new cups to the club in memory of Mr. G. du Temple who had passed away in 1962. The competition for the cup is the same for both mens and ladies. It is to be an 18 hole, medal play, 2-ball competition. Partners are to play to the low handicap of the partner. The Steward Cup format was changed to a more suitable arrangement of play. Ladies regular matches were designated to be played on Tuesdays.

In 1965 the ladies withdrew their funds from the reserve of the parent club and managed it themselves. They started a new "Get Acquainted Match & Tea" competition, which was to be played match play on full handicap.

On the men's side, Mr. Harold Jacobson shot a new course record of 62 for 18 holes. A record that still stands today.

In 1966 the ladies revised the Eclectic competitions again. This time the matches were to be played in 3 levels. Group 1 at 20 Handicap or less, group 2 at 21-29, and group 3 at 30 and over. The parent division purchases a fifty cup urn for use in mixed competitions. Mrs. Steward retired as secretary treasurer after 10 dedicated years.

In 1967 the men revised the "Barr Cup" playoff rules of play to the sudden death format. The ladies have indicated that on Tuesday afternoons, over the winter months, when it is to wet too play golf, Bridge will be played.

In 1968 the first men's LINHGA (Lower Island Nine Hole Golf Association) Inter-Club Competition was played. Mr. Elis Peters, a Metchosin Golf Club member, initiated the competition.

LINHGA was an interclub competition played between Ardmore, Broome Hill (*John Phillips Memorial*), Gregarah (*Prospect Lake*), and Metchosin. *In later years Salt Spring Island and Royal Oak golf clubs join in on the competition.* The entry fee was $10.00 for each club.

The "Barr Trophy" was donated by Captain Barr in memory of his wife to the parent division. The cup is to be played for in a two-ball, 18-hole, mixed format tournament for the "Ball & Chain". (Note: Captain Barr died early in 1969 shortly after the passing of his wife).

The ladies competitions that had always been held in the afternoon were changed in 1969. The games were now to be played in the morning hours. Tournament fees were increased to $3.00.

In 1969, men's button match scoring was revised. The method of scoring was to count the best and second balls on each hole, with an allowance for handicap. Playoffs were decided by sudden death.

Ladies increase the size of their committees. They were as follows: Member in charge of 9-hole competitions (*Mrs. Gwynne is the first to hold this position*), a Convener for teas & lunches, and a Handicap chairperson was appointed. Mrs. Du Temple was to act as ex-officio on all the committees.

In the 1970s the Club continued to grow. The ladies recorded a large increase in the membership in 1971. In 1972 the Constitution and bylaws were rewritten to bring them up to date, incorporating changes to the operations since the last revision. The Club was now forced to pay the fees to the CGLU and RCGA as management decided not to continue forwarding the payments for the Club.

Aerial View of Club House

The Club requested and received approval from management to hold three Sunday, two-ball mixed play tournaments. Tee times were approved for 1:30 pm. Tournament competitors coming off the ninth-hole must alternate with other players starting on the first-hole.

The 'Twilight Foursomes' were running well, with an average 40 men and women in attendance every week.

The ladies had solely managed the event and competitions since they began. The men started to share the responsibilities by alternating with the women every week. The ladies requested, but were denied, a half-hour tee closure to provide them the opportunity to all go off the first tee in a group. This would later be approved.

In 1973 there was an Extraordinary Meeting held on March 7th. The existing executive including the President, Vice- president, Secretary Treasurer, Ladies captain, and Vice-captain all resigned.

A new executive was voted in. The outgoing executive had overextended the Clubs funds and the club was in financial difficulty. Monies had been spent heavily on tournament prizes and other club functions depleting the funds to excess. The new executive was approved by the membership to remove the monies from the Investment Fund purchased years before and place it into the clubs general fund to keep the club running. This executive remained in office for the next three years. The only change was that a new secretary treasurer was elected in 1974. These hard working members got the Club out of the financial woes. In 1975 a new executive was elected. For the first time a woman president was elected. This lady was Mrs. Billie Clement.

The ladies division started a new 'Button Match', with Silver and Bronze challenges. Silver matches were played by those with handicaps of 28 and under, the Bronze matches by those with 29 and over. A new format of officers was set up as follows: Captain, Vice-captain, Sec. Treasurer, Social Committee (nine members), Eclectic Committee (three members), Handicap Committee (three members), Lingha Rep's (two members), and a Rules Committee (three members). In 1976 the 'Ball & Chain' tournament is discontinued.

In 1977 the question was again raised referring to the junior members participating in adult events. It was the general consensus that it's not in the best interest of the juniors or the adults to have them compete in adult competitions. However, the men's captain and vice-captain are to arrange two or three games during the season, between the men and the juniors. The ladies division decides to amalgamate the 'A' and 'B' section for a one-year trial period.

In 1978 it is decided that all new members who joined the men's club (without handicaps) would be given a maximum 24 handicap, until a proper handicap was established. In addition, for all men's division Fixture Competitions, players with higher handicaps were limited to a maximum handicap of 24 for all competitions.

In October, the men decided to separate from the 'Main (Parent) Division and form their own men's division, similar to the ladies. The new division will hold their own competitions, and manage their own finances. The spring of 1979 the men's division was formed. The new division was given a donation of $200.00 by the parent division to cover initial operational costs. A new fixture list was drawn up, and trophies associated with the tournaments were taken over from the parent division. The first men's executives were; Captain: Mr. Edward Ostachowicz, Vice-Captain: Mr. Ron Trelevan, and Sec. Treasurer: Mr. Norm Williams. The first annual meeting was held on October 21st, 1979. Original tournament fees were originally set at $5.00 for the year. This was later dropped and replaced by a $2.00 fee for each tournament except the Club Championship, which was to be a $4.00 fee.

A Men's Day was initiated. After much debate with management the men were permitted to hold a Men's Day each Wednesday. This day was to be used by the members as a get together during the week. Competitions and formats were drawn up for play by the members. However, tournaments on the fixture list were to be played for on Saturdays and Sundays only.

A low-Gross and low-Net prize was added to the list of prizes to be given at the end of each season. To qualify, members must play in at least 50% of Wednesday play.

The handicap limit of 24 is dropped. Members would not be allowed to double up nine-hole scores for handicap purposes. Handicaps were calculated from the results of

Bird Habitat Near The Eighth Green

five 18-hole games or ten 9- hole games.

The Parent Division tournament fixture list was reduced to those mixed competitions, played on Thursday nights and Sundays. Handicaps for Twilight Sixsomes are to be limited to a maximum of 24 for the men and 33 for the ladies.

A new mixed tournament was added to the mixed twilight foursome fixture list. It is the 'Fred Bertouche Trophy' donated in his memory. The competition to be played using alternate drives. Ladies to tee off on the 'odd-holes', and men off on the 'even-holes'.

The ladies changed their Club Championship format from match play to medal play. The winner was established by totaling three combined 18-hole rounds of golf. Runner-up prizes were given out for the first time for the Club Championship, Spring Cup, and Spring Plate. A business ladies section was implemented, to help the women members who were working. The club reinstated the Ladies LINGHA, that had not been played for several few years.

This is the clubs 50th anniversary year, 50 years of continuous trials and tribulation, dedication and many years of great golf. Now, with all that hard work and dedication, and constant improvements to the course and the club times are good times for the club. The men's and ladies divisions had continued to grow in leaps and strides since the mid sixties, and at the beginning of the 80's the Club had never been so large, with over 200 active members. All competitions and functions enjoyed good attendance by both the men's and women's divisions and the Club was prospering. Both divisions were making changes to their competitions, re-arranging the way competitions were being run, and in the method of play, to help ensure all the members were included. In 1980, at the annual meeting and banquet there were 90 men and 83 women in attendance. At this meeting the Constitution and Bylaws was once again amended. In this amendment the Men's Secretary was added to the Executive.

The ladies had several firsts this year. They gave out scripts as prizes for winners of their competitions and runners up. They changed the Club Championship back to the match play format, with a qualifying round and runner up prizes for consolation flights, and the Margaret Rose competition now has pre-draws. Also the ladies paid for part of the banquet costs.

The men had their first 'Mens' Night'. It was set up to get everyone to the Annual General Meeting. Prior to this year the mens' division was having difficulties in getting enough members to attend the annual meeting, so this was an attempt to get participation from the membership. It was a nine-hole competition, followed by a dinner (donated and set-up by the ladies division), and ending with the annual men's division meeting.

Also, since the Twilight Sixsomes began it always concluded with a barbecue but for the first time this tradition would cease.

In 1981 the J.J. White competition between Salt Spring, Pender Island, Galiano, and Ardmore Golf Clubs, started up again, hosted by Ardmore. This competition had ceased during the times when the Ardmore club was having difficulties with management concerning scheduling and fees.

The mixed button match competitions were reinstated again this year. And the Ardmore Thanksgiving Mixed Tournament was played for the second consecutive time.

The ladies division revised their officers to include a New Members Councilor, a Match Chairman, and a publicity officer.

The men's division put in place a 'Hole-in-one' insurance for the members. With this, when a member gets a hole-in-one and it is authenticated by one or more playing members that drinks were purchased, the member would be recompensed up to $20.00 by the men's division.

In 1982 the Twilight Foursomes monies taken in go towards balls as previously done, and that the balls are to be give out the night of competition. The Sunday mixed competitions were set up to include nine-hole competitions for the nine hole members. This year, for the first time, the winners of mixed competitions received 'Take Home' awards, either as trophies or vouchers valued at $5.00. The single members playing for the 'Ball & Chain, cannot win the trophy; it was only for married couples to win. The J.J. White team was selected from a list that was posted one month before the competition. The names on the list were put into a box and drawn for six men and six women to make up the team. The total membership is at 194.

The ladies division adds a 'Birdie Pin' competition, to be won for birdies on par fours and par fives. The ladies course rating is re-rated and set at 67.5.

The Ardmore Golf Club was excluded from the LINHGA competitions because Ardmore management insisted on charging a fee to the players that was higher than the fee charged by the other nine-hole courses, and increased the price of beer and food. Management was also unwilling to close down the first tee to allow players to tee-off together. In time, these problems were solved and Ardmore Golf Course rejoined LINHGA.

In 1983 the selection for the J.J. White competition was changed. The team was selected as couples or pairs, not selected as individual men and women.

The men organized a new Handicap Rules Committee. This committee was to consist of three active members, to review handicaps and to make local rules for men's competitions.

The ladies revised the 'Birdie Pin' competition to include the entire course, not just par fours and fives. Blue pins were given for each birdie up to nine; the tenth pin to be a red pin. A new competition, the Putter Pin, was played for this year. Also new was a pin given to the retiring Captain, each year. It was to be engraved with the name, year, etc.

The ladies division added a telephone committee to the committee list that consisted of six active members.

A new tournament commenced between the Ardmore G.C. and Pender Island G.C.A new trophy was purchased for the competition.

In 1984 an attempt was made to hold the mixed field day competition, normally held on a Thursday evening as part of the Twilight Six-somes schedule, on the first Monday in August at 1:00PM. However, most of the members could not play at that time due to work requirements and other responsibilities. The following year the competition was again reinstated to Thursday night play.

The ladies division found itself low on funds and needed to make changes to cut expenses. As a result the Round Robin fees were raised from 25 cents to 50 cents, yearly dues were raised from $8.00 to $10.00, and the business girls fees were raised from $4.00 to $10.00.

The ladies club added a J.J. White competition to the fixture list. The bridge club, which had been abandoned for a few years, started up again.

The men's division created a new nine-hole division. The committee added a number of new trophies and competitions to the fixture list.

A new barbecue night was started. The first night of play was held on Wednesday, May 30, and continues every last Wednesday of each month throughout the season. Play was to be a nine-hole competition followed by a meal. Tee-off time at 4 PM. The reason behind the new barbecue was to provide the opportunity to have a get together of all the men members to have a fun evening of competition and commeradery. The tee time and nine –hole format are set in this way so no one is excluded, as the intention is to have all members, seven-day, five-day, and nine-holers attend the function. In later years, when membership is expanded to include 'after-three' members the opportunity was extended to include them as well, if they wish to play.

Also new this year, all Men's Division Tournaments were competed for on Wednesdays (Men Days) for the first time. It was as an option to the membership, the standard rule of play was that competitions were to be played on the weekends if possible. Prior to this year all competitions had to be played on weekends only. Members playing in tournaments will be first off the 1st tee, followed by those not in the tournament. Note: This new rule was made due to an increased number of members being in the five-day membership category. As such, they were unable to compete for the trophies. They now have that opportunity.

Two new trophies were donated to the men's division. The first was the 'Beaton Trophy'

donated by Mr.Les Beaton. The trophy to go to the winner of the 'C' Flight, of the Club Championship. Mr. Joe Flint also donates a trophy. It was to go to winners of the Low Gross and Low Net awards based on Wednesday (Men's Day) play.

1985. The twilight Sixsomes added to the prizes, one ball, for 'Low Gross' team for that night. The 'Field Day' was to remain to be played on Thursday nights, as man-agement will not permit the competition to move to another day or time.

The golf course rating was re-evaluated once again this year. The Men's rating became 64, and the Ladies changed to 68.5. Total membership stood at 91 men and 98 women at the close of the year.

The club championship method of play was altered to the 'Match Play' format.

1987. The club held an Extraordinary Meeting on January 27th, with 47 members present, to revise the Constitution and Bylaws to include the nine-hole Captain as members of the Executive.

The parent division, for the first time this year gave out trophies/ vouchers to the winners of the Twilight Sixsome 'field day' competitions. These include the long drives, aggregate long drive, and the pitch and putt, for both men and women. Also, for the first time, all mixed and pair tournament winners are to defend their titles the following year.

A new rules committee was formed consisting of a Chairperson, the Men's and Ladies Captains, the men's Vice-captain, the ladies Rules Chairperson, and one other member as selected by the Chairperson.

The men held a special meeting on March 25th, concerning continued participation in the LINHGA competitions. Ardmore management would charge the men's club for one-half the cost of green fees for players from visiting teams. The men's treasurer would reimburse the full fees to Ardmore on behalf of visiting players hosted at home. This cost was retroactive to the beginning of the Andy MacGregor Matches.

An Extraordinary Meeting was held on July 26th, to discuss disciplinary action to be taken against a Club Member. He was a very unruly, unpleasant person, known for throwing his clubs and using foul language during play. The situation had become so bad that other members, both men and women, do not wish to have him play in their groups. He had been approached several times by the club to clean up his act, to no avail. It was decided that the Club Member was to be suspended from competitive play for 30 days, essentially the remainder of the '87' season. He would be reinstated the following year. A letter was sent to the individual informing him of the clubs decision. *(Note: This person never did return, giving up his memberships to the Course and Club)*

The men's division finances were in a deficit of 112% at the year's end. This was due mainly to the additional LINHGA/ Andy MacGregor fees, which added a $270 burden to the division. In order to pay the deficit and ensure monies for the following year, Wednesday fees are increased to $1.00 per tournament. The Andy MacGregor costs next year will be paid out the men's general fund.

1988 the Constitution and Bylaws were amended again to make changes to the overall structure of the document. The total membership at the end of the year is at 208 members.

The men's division discontinues the 'Button Matches' due to the lack of interest by the membership.

The nine-hole club revised their rules set-up to conform within the guidelines of the 18-hole club.

A Junior Championship was again formed, for the first time since 1977. The tournament was to be a 36-hole competition played using the stroke play format. A trophy, to be known as the du Temple Trophy, was to be purchased by the management. The men's division were purchase the keeper trophies, to be given to the winner each year.

The rules for the Barr Trophy at the time it was donated stipulated that competitors must have played in at least three Twilight Sixsome nights to qualify to play for the Cup. The ruling had been removed from the competition a few years earlier but in 1989 it was again reinstated back into the rules. The Club sets up a new set of rules for breaking ties in the field day competitions. They are as follows. Long drive: to be broken by one drive, Pitch & Putt: to be broken by one pitch and putt.

The club once again initiated a nine-hole tournament to be played in conjunction with Sunday 18-hole

Bird Habitat Near The Ninth Fairway

tournaments. *(Writer note: this has never had participation from the nine-holers and as such has never been played).*

The men reinstated the Fall Cup to their fixture list. The competition to be played from October 15th to March of the following year. The Eclectic, which was a monthly competition throughout the playing season, was removed from the fixture list due to the lack of interest from the membership.

In 1991 the Parent Division had excess monies in the club fund. It donated $200 each to the Men's and Ladies Divisions. The membership dues were increased to $18/ year for the following years to cover the increase in dues by the RCGA and CGLU.

There was some dissention in the Ladies Division. It arose from differences of opinion between the 9-hole and 18-hole groups as to how things should operate, resulting in the 9-hole members asking to form their own division. After consultation and a visit from the Zone President, it was determined that the CLGA will not permit a separate entity, that they must operate under the umbrella of the 18-hole group and report to them. They are permitted to elect their own executive with a Convener rather than a Captain, and draw up their own schedule/ fixture list , and fees to be paid to the 18-hole treasurer. (Some funding was provided by the Ladies Club.) The 9-hole Margaret Rose, and the Button Matches are to go to the 9-hole division. The 9-hole Round Robin is to remain a mixed event.

The ladies made some changes to their competitions. Birdie pins were given out to the player with the most accumulated birdies for the month, one for each month of the playing season. All players were eligible to qualify for the 'Spring Cup', the 'A' and 'B' divisions are removed from play. All the ladies had to be members of the CLGA and all the members must pay the membership.

A new trophy was donated to the ladies division. The Valentine Rose Bowl (a silver bowl) was donated by Isabel Valentine in memory of her husband Len. The Bowl was meant to replace the Margaret Rose Trophy. The format of play is to remain as is, that being the total score accumulated from the three best scores taken from five 18-hole games.

The men passed a ruling regarding the participation of members in competitions. Members were finding it difficult to set up matches with members in other categories. For example, a seven-day member is to play a five-day member. The five-day member makes it difficult, not wishing to co-operate with the seven-day member, to arrange a time to play. He then insists that the seven-day member must forfeit the match because the five-day member is rated higher in the competition. The new rule states that seven-day members take precedence, followed by five-day members, and finally the after-three members.

In 1992 at the annual general meeting the Constitution and Bylaws were read to the membership for clarification. The membership accepts them as written.

A computer was purchased for use by the membership. Members can now keep track of their handicaps by entering their scores into the computer. The program permits entries of scores from other clubs.

In 1993 the "Barr Cup" rules of play were changed once again. The requirement that players must play in three Twilight Sixsome evenings to qualify to play in the competition has again been removed.

The ladies designed a new putter pin to give out as prizes for that competition. It is decided that all tournaments on the fixture list will be played with all handicap levels playing together, not in handicap divisions. The only exceptions are the 'Club Championship', and all CLGA games as they must be played in handicap divisions.

1994. The BCGA have changed the way scores are recorded. The association has, over the years, noted an unfair discrepancy of handicaps between golf clubs due to the course ratings. That is to say that members playing out of a less difficult course were required to use that handicap when they competed at a more difficult course, putting them at a real disadvantage. This year the BCGA has introduced the slope system, which brings the play between players from other courses on to a more level playing field. It removes the 'handicap' and replaces it with the 'index'. The 'index' is calculated using the member's scores, course rating, and slope rating. The slope rating identifies the difficulty of the course. Each course has an 'index list'. Players from other courses find their 'index number' on this list, and their handicap is converted. All golf courses are given a handicap rating and a slope rating. As a part of this change the Ardmore golf course men's rating is reviewed and given a new rating of 64.6, and a slope rating of 101.

In 1994 the BCGA, Island Chapter, held a golf tournament known as the 'Golf 100' to commemorate 100 years of golf on the island. The tournament was sponsored by the Post Office, and was held at the Victoria Golf Club, noted as the oldest course in British Columbia. The tournament was such a success it became a yearly competition. Teams, consisted of three men and three women, from each club. The method of play was the scramble format. The tournament continued for the next three years until sponsorship was lost.

A new trophy was presented to the Ladies Division by Mrs. Jean Streeter, to be played for in conjunction with the five Valentine Rose Bowl games and awarded for the lowest number of putts using the best three of the five games.

The Parent Division sent letters to the Ardmore management with the intent to start up a new tournament. The proposal suggests a mixed open tournament to be played by both Ardmore members and members from other clubs. The tournament would be run and managed by the Ardmore Golf Club. Four letters were sent to the Ardmore Board of Directors, and the president had several discussions with management, however the club never got a response from management.

In 1995 the men added a new competition to the fixture list. Actually this was a reinstated competition which was not played for several years. After a review changes were made to the time of play. It was decided to reinstate the 'Men's Eclectic' and 'Round Robin' competitions. The rules of play to be that both are to be played over the winter months from October to March of each year. Scores for both competitions to be recorded on lists provided. Members with the most overall wins in the 'round robin' win a trophy at the end of the year. Those with the lowest round in the eclectic also win a trophy. In 1998 it was decided to play the eclectic in divisions to make the competition fairer to all players.

1996. The BCGA increased its dues and as a result the Ardmore Club increased its dues to compensate. Dues were increased to $25 for the ladies and $21 for the men.

A new trophy was donated to the men's division to be added to the fixture list. The trophy, donated by Mr. Murray Matheson, is to go to the 'Most Improved Player of the Year' determined by using the index rating.

1997. The club changed the fee structure for the Twilight Foursomes. In place of the different charges for special events, a fee of $1.00 was charged at all evening and Sunday competitions. There was no fee charged for the Men versus Women competition.

1998. A new computer was purchased and a place provided alongside so people can sit comfortably while entering their score.

1999. The course rating was re-assessed by the BCLGA District #1 changing it from 69.4 to 68.6, with a slope of 112 for the ladies. The men's section expressed thanks to the course management for the changes made during the year.

2000. Men's Division revamped rules of play for competitions. This is required so as to accommodate the larger membership which is now at 86 members. A weekly 'Putting Competition' was introduced with scores to be recorded during regular tournament play on men's day. The monthly evening barbeques have been changed to daytime events. It will follow the 18 holes of play in the morning.

A new trophy, the 'Millennium Trophy', donated by Mr. Eric Airey, was introduced for the mixed Twilight Sixsomes. Rules of play - as a team competition using the 'Texas Scramble' format.

The course had been improved by extending/ adding to the cart paths so that all the holes are accessible all year long for those requiring the use of carts.

The Annual Banquet was held at Theo's Restaurant located in Sidney.

2001. The Men's membership was strong with 91 members, 14 in the hole-hole division. A new trophy was donated to the Ladies Division by Mrs. Emily Young, to be awarded to the lowest average net score over a number of specified competitions. The first winner of this prestigious trophy was Mrs. Julia Toller. The Twilight sixsomes have been seeing from 12 to 40 members on Thursday nights

2002. The Ladies Division sent 15 members to a District Annual Rules Workshop. They host the District Net Tournament and the LINHGA Fall Field Day. They marked the 50th anniversary of continuous Interclub play with the ladies at Cowichan Golf Club, and played in the annual interclub with Pender Island with Ardmore winning the trophy. Also competed in the Metchosin Field Day, District Net Tournament, March Meadows Field Day, Snr. Ladies Field Day, and District Foursomes. They have provided additional play by introducing the 'B.C.Pin', 'Yellowball', and 'Tombstone' competitions Sadly, they announce the disbanding of the 9-hole Section due to a severe drop in membership.

The Men's Division introduced a new trophy, the 'Net Champion' trophy, which was played as part of the Club Championship. Some existing trophies which were in need of repair have had the work done.

The Constitution and Bylaws were updated. The computer program handicap software was upgraded to meet with RCGA approval.

Course improvement includes the extension of the No. 6 tee, making the hole longer, necessitating the need to make a par four from the back location. Golf Lesson Facility between holes three and four fairways will have netting installed to protect players on the course.

2003. The Ladies Division had the course re-rated. New rating went from a 68.6 to 69.9 with a slope from 112 to 117. They announce they have 41 playing members attending ladies day events.

The Parent Division announced the decline of participation by the members in the Twilight Sixsomes competitions. Some nights there are only 10 to 12 players in attendance. It may soon become necessary to delete the events from the schedule.

2004. Men's Division have had the course re-rated for men's play. The course was rated at 64.7, with a slope of 100. New rating is 32.6, with a 105 slope - for the front nine, and a rating of 32.8, with a 101 slope – back nine. Overall slope rated at 103.

2005. The Ladies Division announce the CLGA and BCLGA have been changed to the RCGA and BCGA respectfully, and instead of being in a 'District' we are now in 'Zone 5'.

The President expressed his disappointment in the lack of interest of members in the Twilight Sixsome activities and that the J.J. White Interclub Tournament, which was started by our club, was not supported by our members and our participation had to be cancelled.

A newer computer was donated by one of the men's members and a printer by a ladies member. The course has had a website for some time now and we will ask to have the fixture lists added to the site. The course management has been asked make club dues mandatory for all new members. A change of note to the course layout is the addition of a new bunker on left side of the fairway on Hole NO.3.

2006. The ladies had 34 participating members. The course management had taken over the administration of membership affiliations with BCGA and collected all Club affiliation fees. The amount of $20.00 per member, from the yearly fee was paid to the Golf Club, with $10 per member going to the Parent Division, and $10 per member, to the Men's and Ladies Divisions.

The 'Bill Smith' Pro-Am Tournament, having been played for a couple of years, was added to the fixture list as a regular event, to be played at the middle of July. Format to be a nine-hole scramble. Trophy and Prizes were provided by the course management.

2007. The ladies had 36 active members, and the men average 80. The men make a change in the fixture list by delaying start times in early spring and late fall months by one-half hour, to give more sunlight and warmth for play.

A new course-owned computer system has been installed for use by all members for entering handicaps, booking tee times, etc. In addition the course opens a restaurant called the 'Iron Grill'. The Club decided to hold a monthly barbecue that would be catered by this facility.

2008. The men's division had 83 active members, averaging 46 on men's day and four to six nine-holers. The newly revised Constitution and By-Laws was accepted by the Registrar of Companies dated 10 Oct 08.

2009. A newly revised Constitution and Bylaws had been adopted, and the format had been changed significantly (with the hope that it would assist in bringing the Club's Divisions closer together as one) and simplifying the management structure of the club. The club entered the computer age as well and purchased the necessary software programs.

Colour and Cover

Chapter Seventeen:

Golf Course Layout

The course layout has changed over the years. Description of each hole will attempt to depict the present day layout (2012) and a comparison of previous years as changes were made.

The First and Tenth Tee at Ardmore

Hole No. 1 & 10

Today

A 295/310 par 4, with a slight dogleg to the left, guarded on the left by trees and bunker approx. 220 yards from the Tee, and 2 fir trees to right side of the green. There is a Sensitive Area (ESA) upper right side of fairway which is Out of Bounds.

There are 2 teeing areas along with red and white tee markers. Red for front nine & white for back nine.

Previously

In the seventies this hole was a 345yard par 4. The tee was located closer to the present parking lot, in the general area of the practice green. The right side of the fairway was fenced off, to keep animals penned. A ball landing in the penned area was Out of Bounds.

In the early 2000's two fir trees to right side of the green fell in a heavy rain storm.

First and Tenth Tee at Ardmore

The Second and Eleventh Tee At Ardmore

Hole No. 2 & 11

Today

A par 5, playing 475/459 yds, with a dogleg to the right, the green is guarded by 2 fir trees in front. The tee shot is approx. 200 yards to the dogleg, guarded by 'Out of Bounds' stakes on both sides of the fairway to the end of the dog leg. Also by a tree & bush lined ditch on the right at the end of the dogleg, and a line of trees along the right side with a sand bunker at the corner and another at the far side of the dogleg. The 'Out-of-Bounds', treed and bushed, continues along the right side of the fairway, from the corner of the dogleg to the right side of the green The tee is 2 tiered, with the lower level at the front. No.11 tees on the lower level, and No.2 tees on the top tier.

Previously

In the 70's this was hole No.6, a 525 yard par 5. The distance was slightly shorter to the dogleg with the tee located beside the oak tree to the left of the present tee. The distance of the green has been shortened with the addition of a new green in its present location. The old No.6 & 11 hole green is the now used as No.5 green. The trees lining the right side of the fairway to the corner of the dogleg were planted in the late 70's.

Hole No.3 & 12

Today

A par 4, playing at 328/340 yds, straight away. No out of bounds. A pond forms in a lower area located between No.3 & 4 hole fairways, adjacent the 150-yard marker. The green is protected on the left by a large Sequoya tree. The fairway is also tree lined starting 30 yds from the tee. Tee is 2 tiered with alternate tees for No. 3 & 12. No.3 on the bottom & 12 on the top tier.

Note: There is a practise green located 75 yards to the right of No.3 green. This green is used by the golf professional for lessons. When not in use for lessons members may enjoy it.

In the 70's this was hole No.7, playing at 315 yards. Yardage was shorter with the tee located 15 yards ahead of its present location.

The Third and Twelfth Fairway At Ardmore

Hole No.4 & 13

Today

A straight away, par 4, playing 384/397 yds. Out-of-bounds on the left side, beyond the boundary fence, from tee to green. There is a grouping of trees on the right side of the fairway, starting adjacent to the 150-yard markers and pond between the 3rd and 4th fairways. Also on the right side of the fairway, near the green, is a group of larger more mature trees. There are bunkers located just after the 150 yd markers on both sides of the fairway. There is also a bunker located 4 yds to the rear left of the green.

Previously

In the70's this was hole No.8. It was a 419 yd par 5, with the tee set back, left, into the trees some 25 yards back from where the tee is presently located. The group of trees on the right were planted in the late 70's by the grounds keeper Mr. Archie McCulloch. There was an oak tree located at the back right side of the green which fell onto the green during a storm in the early 90's.

Note: There is a structure located approx. 50 yards to the right of the 150 yd marker on No 4 fairway, between holes No.3 & 4. that is used for storage and golf instruction. A driving net is installed and a small practice area and sand trap is available for swing improvements.

The Fourth and Thirteenth Fairway At Ardmore

Hole No.5 & 14

Today

A par 3, playing 110/102 yards, straight away. Out-of-bounds beyond the maintenance yard fence to the left side. Guarded by large oak trees on the left and right side of the fairway, with overhanging branches. Bunker located at the back of the green. Slightly raise tee area with 2 sets of tees for front & back. Green slopes gradually the tee from front to back. *Note: This was the old No.6 green, or present day No.2&10.*

Previously

In the 70's this hole did not exist. The Hole No.9 was an entirely different hole in an entirely different location. It was a par 3, playing 137 yards. The original hole was taken out of play in the 80's when the present No.5&14 hole was constructed. The original hole ran along Ardmore Rd. The tee was located at the corner of Ardmore & West Saanich Rds, in the general area of the present bunker behind the present No.4&13 hole.

The green was located between where the present No.5&14 tee is located and perimeter fence at the parking. The right side was guarded by a large oak tree, midway up the fairway, which fell in the 90's. The left side was 'Out-of-Bounds' beyond the perimeter fence along Ardmore road, for the entire length of the hole. At the rear of the tee was a covered sitting bench with an 'Ardmore Golf Course' sign.

The Fifth and Fourteenth Fairway At Ardmore

Hole No.6 & 15

<u>Today</u>

Hole No.6 plays as a par 4, playing 251 yards, straight away, from the back tee. 'Out-of-Bounds' along the left side, outside the perimeter fence, from tee to green, and the property fence, behind and to the left of the green. There is a bunker located at the rear of the green, to the right. The green is partially tiered with no relatively flat areas and is heavily sloped from right to left. The tee area is deep, and the front tee plays as a par 3, playing approx. 231 yds , for hole No.15. The tee area has a protective fence along the right side. The back tees are guarded by tall, well established trees located 20yds to front, on both sides forming a chute in which to come through with the tee shot.

<u>Previously</u>

In the 70's this was hole No.3. It was a par 3, 230 yards. The tee was located in front of the present pathway where you cross over the creek. There was a teeing mat located just back from the creek. The tee shot was through a narrow chute of trees on both sides. *<u>Note:</u> The scars can still be seen on the oak tree to the right from all the balls driven into it over the years.* The green was partially rebuilt in the late 90's, to level it out a little. It was guarded by a fairway bunker on the right side, approx.165 yds from the tee, a bunker adjacent to the green on the left side, and another below the tall trees to the left of the green approx. 40yds away. There were also 2 trees located to the left of the green tall enough to cause concern if a ball went left of the green.

<u>Note:</u> *This hole was designated as the most difficult par 3 in British Columbia.*

Hole No.7 & 16

Today

This is a par 4 of 294 yards. It is a ninety degree dogleg to the left. An accurate tee shot of 190 yards is needed. The left side of the fairway is lined with over hanging oak trees. The famous Du Temple oak stands at the corner. Weeping willows line the left side beneath the reservoir walls. Any shots to the right or the left are in great peril and accuracy in distance is required. The green slopes more than is apparent from back to front.

Previously

In the 70's this was hole No.3, playing at 290 yds. The tee has been improved by adding a pro-tective fence on the right side. The ditch on the left was deepened to improve drainage. There was a penned area on the left side with structures used to house the donkeys. The area beyond the fence was 'Out-of-Bounds'. It was removed in the 80's, and is now an open field. The reservoir at the rear and right side of the dogleg was constructed in the late 70's. At the base of the reservoir, before the perimeter fence, was an open ditch known as a 'Scotch Drain'. Balls landing in the Scotch Drain could be removed, and dropped, with no penalty. This drain was covered over in the late 90's. Also around this time additional drainage was installed in the fairway from the dogleg to the green to help remove severe puddling from the area. In the early

2000's some trees located on the right side of the fairway, at the dogleg, blew over in a severe storm.

The Seventh and Sixteenth Fairway At Ardmore

The Eighth and Seventeenth Fairway at Ardmore

Hole No.8

Today

A par 3, 139/155 yds long, straightaway. Guarded by 3 bunkers, 1 to the right side of the fairway ahead of the green, another 15 yards over on the right parallel with the green, and another 7 yards behind the green. A pond runs along the entire length of the green and beyond approx. 7 to 8 yds distance away. At the front of the pond is a gazebo which houses a water pump. The tee area is 2 tiered, and elevated. No.8 tees are located on the lower level, and No.17 tees on the top tier.

Previously

In the 70's this was Hole No. 5, playing at 137 yds. The tee was a rubber mat located to the right of the present lower tier tee, where the cart path is located. The bunkers on the left hand side and rear of the green were put in during the early 90's. There was a fence along the left side of the fairway, where the field is now, which was used to keep the donkeys This area was Out-of-Bounds, however, you could retrieve your ball by climbing a specially constructed set of steps, over the fence.

Hole No.17

Fairway # 17 plays across the two ponds seen in the photo. The elevated grass tee can be seen at the top of the photo with a cart path leading down to a willow. An accurate shot of between 85 and 95 yards is required. Bunkers back of the green penalize shots that are too long. A shot out of one of those bunkers that is too long could hit water. This is a beautiful golf hole that requires control of both mind and swing.

Hole No.9 & 18

Today

A par 4, playing 381/374 yds, straightaway. The right side has trees and 2 reservoirs along the fairway. A pump house is located on the slope from the largest reservoir, 190 yards from the tee, on the right. All the slopes of the reservoirs are now formidable natural hazards. Adjacent to the slope of the large reservoir, before the No. 6 tee, is a small pond located in the level area. The fairway has 2 bunkers, 1 on each side, just beyond the 150 yd markers. The green is guarded in front by 2 bunkers, one at each corner, and just in front of them the fairway dips down and up again from a distance of approx 30 yds. To the left of the green is a small grass mogul. There is a protective fence behind the green to stop balls from going long. Balls clearing the fence are 'Out-of-Bounds'.

Previously

In the 70's this was Hole No.2, playing 394 yds. The tee area was set back into the hill, approx. where the back tier of No.2 is now, at a much lower level. It was guarded by a couple of large oak trees on the left side which could catch a tee shot. One blew down in the early 80's, and the other chopped down soon after. The tee was then raised and leveled. In the 80's the newest & largest reservoir was constructed. A bunker, shaped like a donkey, in front of the green was altered into 2 bunkers, removing the middle section. In the 90's the right side bunker was removed and replaced with the present deep bunker and the left side bunker has been deepened and enlarged as well. Another bunker located to the left side, parallel with the green, has been landscaped into a grass mogul. The bunkers at the 150 yd markers were added in the 2000's.

The Ninth and Eighteenth Fairway at Ardmore From Green

Chapter Eighteen

The Unexpurgated Facts: Fitness, Failure and Donkey Danger

When Mrs. Alice Du Temple died on Sept 17th, 1984 she left a will that transferred equal voting power to Barry and Wally Du Temple. No voting shares were willed to her daughter in-law, Betty Du Temple. This was a recipe for corporate dysfunction and for a family upheaval that didn't fail. The brothers would either have to agree or one would need to acquiesce in order to make business decisions.

In 1985 my brother Barry George Du Temple became ill from a severe case of osteoporosis. The onset had taken several years but had become very noticeable while he was a principal of an elementary school in Quesnel. He needed to consult specialists in Vancouver, Victoria and Seattle. He wanted to come home and to co-manage the Ardmore Golf Course during his 'recovery'. As an equal holder of the voting shares he could do that. Unfortunately one crisis led to another. Barry fell into a deep depression. He had started to drink heavily in Quesnel and now rapidly became a full high flying alcoholic. I tried to help but unknowingly became an enabler who tried to hide the facts from the public, and made excuses for my brother. Finally Barry 'came out of the closet' as one says, and declared that he was gay. Did I accept it? He wanted to see how I would react. This was at a time when 'homophobia' was extreme in society. He said that he would never have told his Mom or Dad, and had hidden it for years. He wanted always to get smaller whenever some hint of the subject of being gay came up. He blamed other people for his drinking because of how they denigrate gays. He hated his parents for having tried to be matchmakers for him. He hated the fact that he had played along, and gone out with girls to please his parents. It was like they knew something and thought that they could fix him. Now he was getting smaller. Were the decades of repression, of hiding his orientation the cause of his drinking and bone

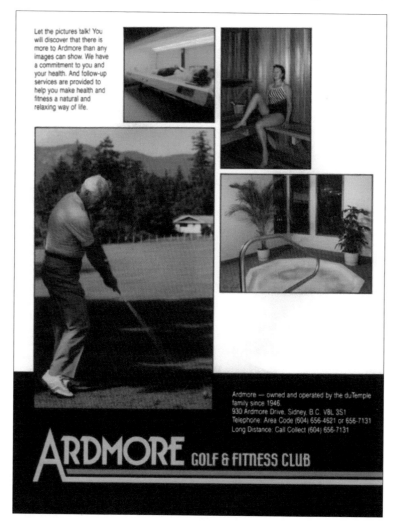

deterioration? As a brother I listened and gave love and support. I accepted him and his orientation. When he would not go to classes designed for 'gay orientation' or to the psychiatrist for the 'depression', or to the recovery seminars for 'alcoholism' I attended with him.

It was during this time period that my brother Barry commissioned a study to see whether there was a need for a health club in the area. Could a health club be viable as part of the golf course experience? He first proposed to expand the building at Ardmore so that golfers could use the health club before or after playing. However, the needs and feasibility report indicated that the health club should be located in Sidney. I agreed with Barry to proceed with a renovation of a rented space in the Sidney Mall. I thought that perhaps his full attention on the new business would make things better at the golf course. The facility was named The Ardmore Golf and Fitness Club. Members of the health club were given free golf at Ardmore Golf Course after 3 pm Mondays to Fridays with an option to become full members. Full members at Ardmore could use the facility whenever they wished. The fitness club became a financial burden when not enough members registered to pay expenses. With much difficulty I convinced Barry that we had to close shop. We sold the equipment, and made full refunds for any memberships still outstanding. The after 3 pm memberships that exist at Ardmore today are a result of that history.

The failure of the 'Fitness Centre' compounded the problems created by Barry's health. He had taken a personal interest in managing it. When I was successful in twisting Barry's arm to help me close it, Barry fell into an even deeper depression and drank to toxic alcohol overload daily. I became heavily stressed. I had to manage the golf course but all too often I needed to assist my brother home, after removing him from a ditch or a pond, undress him, and put him into bed. Then I had to be at the golf course the next morning for opening. I also wanted to have a normal family life with my wife and two children. After my hospitalization I joined 'Al-anon' a society for the friends and relatives of alcoholics. I learned that I had become an enabler and that I should take severe measures so that Barry would finally seek help. I decided on

At Ardmore we believe that good health is your best investment, more important than any financial program. Our professional staff design tailor-made fitness and recreational programs to help make and keep you healthy.
Our Keiser Pneumatic Resistance machines are better than any other exercise product and can be used safely for therapeutic recovery, strength building or endurance conditioning. Our 9-hole golf course is beautiful and challenging twelve months of the year.

a course of 'tough love'. I decided to use every method I could think of to force him into 'rehabilitation'. Members and green fee players had become all too aware of the disorder in the clubhouse office, pro-shop and lounge. My health was suffering as well.

The Times Colonist published the following article about the nerve-wracking events, tensions, and problems at Ardmore Golf Course during this period.

From The Times Colonist 10.05 1987
Brother Tried To Help

A 50-year-old man changed his plea to guilty in an impaired driving case, described as "bizarre" by both Crown and defence counsel in Sidney Provincial Court on Thursday.

Barry George du Temple part-owner of Ardmore Golf and Fitness Club, was found in his car with the keys in the ignition by Sidney RCMP on the Ardmore property last fall. His brother Wally had notified police that Barry was attempting to drive.

Wally told the court that he had tried persistently to prevent Barry from drinking and driving.

Defense counsel Barry Mah Ming said Wally had imposed a fine system on his alcoholic brother every time he did not show up or was late for work at the club's pro shop. Barry would have to donate $500.00 to a registered charity.

In addition, Wally would remove the ignition keys in golf carts so Barry could not drive them on the roads.

Mah Ming said the situation was, in part, caused by Barry's severe osteoporosis, a bone disorder, which has resulted in the loss of nine inches in height over the past six years. Du Temple's neck and part of his chest has disappeared because of the spinal collapse.

"It has been a difficult situation," said Mah Ming. "With the handicap for the last number of years, he chose an ineffective solution by wallowing in self pity; and alcohol became a means of escape." Realizing his condition du Temple joined Alcoholics Anonymous and enrolled in a series of three Excellence courses designed to raise self esteem, said his lawyer. His brother Wally attended many of the sessions with du Temple.

The accused spent $6,000 on treatments and lost $9000 in wages," said Mah Ming.

For his second impaired driving conviction, Judge Robert Greig banned du Temple from driving for nine months and fined him $500 payable by July 31."

Barry du Temple joined AA and continued on the path of 'one day at a time'. He had accepted his own sexual orientation and no longer tried to hide it. With medications and without alcohol he in fact lived a happier life for many years. He became an outstanding Commander of the Saanich Peninsula Power Squadron whose members remember his accomplishments. He took up cruising with the Holland America Line and became a valued volunteer as an instructor of boating courses of advanced navigation.

However, I had lost my brother forever as a friend. If ever a phrase can be a knife the accusation that I was 'a disloyal brother' sunk deep into my flesh. We had almost died together while running rapids in the Grand Canyon of the Liard. We had been closer than most brothers ever get. Now all was shattered.

Barry decided to use his equal voting power to disrupt the functioning of the company. Bills and employees could not be paid. In a court case a judge ruled that since disagreements were making the company dysfunctional an equal number of voting shares would be distributed between Betty, Barry and Wally Du Temple. Next all shareholders signed an agreement that stated that none of the Du Temples or their relatives would be allowed to work on the property as employees but would operate the course through managers. Ardmore Golf Course would be run as a first class operation with qualified and trained staff from that point onward.

But emotional consequences were still to follow the rearrangement. Barry issued an eviction notice for removal of the donkeys from the golf course forthwith. If I couldn't move them he would euthanized them. I pleaded that I had no place to put the donkeys. A group of members and green fees that loved the donkeys launched a 'Save The Ardmore Donkey' campaign that reached into newspaper and radio media. The public outcry was about to explode. It threatened to be bigger than saving the bunny rabbits at the University of Victoria or stopping a deer cull. The problem was avoided thanks to the good hearted action of Betty Du Temple who announced that the donkeys could live out their natural lives at Ardmore, with the restrictions that no more donkeys be brought onto the property, and that all expenses for the care of the donkeys would be the responsibility of Wally du Temple. Could most of the emotional gyrations, fraternal fights and business experiments have been avoided by a deciding vote of Betty Du Temple? The donkeys lived happily into retirement and old age with golfers feeding them to plumpness: Indra, Flipper, Randy, Buttercup, Nadene, Ebony, Ardmore, Bailey, Pancha and Mancha, and Thumper the mule.

Barry died from a collapsed spine on August 4th, 1997. A huge celebration of his life in the clubhouse allowed me to orate about our good times together. His cremains remain in an urn on my library shelf like a complicated but unique read that has yet more hidden secrets. His spirit still lingers in the clubhouse at sunset when you become aware that someone was there when a shadow seems to move the air in passing.

Appendix A:

Ardmore Golf Club Tournament Trophies, Origin and Rules of Play (to 2010)

The Spring Cup

<u>Donated:</u> In 1957

<u>Rules of play:</u> Nine hole, Scotch 2-ball, competition. Alternate drives on every hole, and continue alternate shot until hole is completed, using ¾ combined handicap. Ties will be broken by retrogression. Champions to play together the following year in defense of their title.

The Fred Bertouche Trophy

<u>Donated:</u> in 1979 by Mrs. Bertouche in memory of Fred.

<u>Rules of Play:</u> To be played by alternate drives. Ladies tee off on the 'odd holes', and men tee off the 'even holes'. Play continues using alternate shots until hole is completed. Total strokes of the 2 partners, minus their handicaps,

The Field Day Trophies

Long Drive – Ladies Donated: In 1933
Long Drive – Men Donated: In 1951
Aggregate Drives - Ladies Donated: In 1987
Aggregate Drives – Men Donated: In 1987
Pitch & Putt – Ladies Donated: In 1977
Pitch & Putt – Men Donated: In 1926

du Temple *and* Ostachowicz

The "Ball & Chain" Barr Cup

Donated: In 1959 by Capt.& Mrs. Barr.

Rules of Play: Competition by married couples only. 18 hole, 2-ball, alternate shot, until hole is completed, using ½ combined handicap. Team must alternate tee shots. Ties will be broken by retrogression.

The "Odds & Sods" Stacey Trophy

Donated: in 1986 by Elizabeth Stacey in memory of her husband. She was the sister of Les Beaton a well known member.

Rules of Play: Same as the 'Ball & Chain', with competition by couples who are not married to each other.

The Millennium Trophy

Donated: In 2000 by Mr. Eric Aire to welcome in the new century.

Rules of play: Teams consisting of 2 men & 2 women using the 'Texas Scramble' format.

The "Men vs. Women" Plaque

Purchased by the Club:

Rules of Play: 18 hole competition between the men and women divisions using match play. Men give the women an added 5 strokes plus the difference in handicaps. Captains must play each other. All other players will have handicaps matched as close as possible. In case of am tie the 2 captains play sudden death. Scoring:1 point to the person winning the most holes on the front 9, another1 point for the person winning the most holes on the back 9, and another1 point for the person winning the most holes overall, totaling 3 points.

The Norm Williams Memorial

Donated: In 1984 by Ethel Williams in memory of her husband a favorite club member.

Rules of play: Nine hole, a best- ball (a revised Scotch 2-ball) competition. Everyone drives on every hole, then use the best ball as chosen, and continue alternate shot from that location until hole is completed, using $\frac{1}{4}$ combined handicap. Ties will be broken by retrogression.

The Barr Trophy

Donated: by Captain Barr in 1968 in memory of Mrs. Barr.

Rules of Play: 18 hole, 2-ball, alternate shot, until hole is completed, using 1/2 combined handicap. Team must alternate tee shots. Ties will be broken by retrogression. Champions to play together the following year in defense of their title.

The Winter Mixer

Donated: In 1971

Rules of Play: A 9 hole, revised Stableford, par competition. Team consisting of 1 man and 1 woman. Each partner plays own ball, scoring points playing to his or her own par, according to their handicaps. Partners add their point together on each hole. Highest point total wins. Scoring: 5 pts for a Hole-in-one, 4 pts for an Eagle, 3 pts for a Birdie, 2 pts for a Par, and 1 pt. for a Bogie. Ties are broken by the number of points won on the last three holes. If needed go back 4 holes, then 5 holes, etc. Handicaps to be rounded up to the next full number. (i.e. 11 $\frac{1}{2}$ goes up to 12). Champions to play together the following year in defense of their title.

The Inter-Club Mixed Event

The J.J. White Inter Club Trophy

Donated: In 1929 by Mr. J. J. White.

Rules of Play: This is an 18 hole event played between Ardmore and Gulf Island golf clubs. Each Club submits a team of 12 players, six ladies & six men. Play is stroke play on team combined handicaps. The winning club is determined by adding together the best 4 low net Ladies scores and the best 4 low net Men's scores. In the event of a tie, all six scores are used.

Men's Division Events

The Captain's Spring Cup

Donated: In 1928.

Rules of Play: Stroke play with current handicaps at time of play over two 18-hole rounds as scheduled. Weekend players are urged to complete their rounds on Wednesday but, if unable, should be played on the preceding Sunday. Ties to be broken by an 18-hole playoff within seven days of the completion of the second round of the tournament at a mutually agreed date, excepting Wednesday. Should competitors still be tied after this round a winner will be decided by playing off hole by hole (RCGA Rules of Golf, Rule 33-6 and Appendix I, Section 11)

The G.W. du Temple Memorial Trophy

Donated: In 1964 by the duTemple family in memory of Mr. George duTemple.

Rules of Play: Player must have a valid Men's Club handicap (minimum of 5 recorded scores). Two-man team, best ball, net score. The lowest score (best ball) is the team's score for each hole. One 18-hole round as scheduled. Choose your own partner but there can be <u>no more than five strokes between team members.</u> Names of each team are to be submitted to the Club Captain <u>one week</u> prior to the tournament. Handicaps of each team are averaged based on current handicaps. If the average calculates to a half-fraction round up to next whole number. Ties will be broken by matching cards (RCGA Rules of Golf, Appendix I, Section 11).

The Gamble Cup

Donated: In 1901

Rules of Play: Match play with current handicaps at time of play. This competition is open to a maximum of 64 members and will be played over the Spring/Summer period. After the first match draw the players that fall out of this round will be placed in the second flight. Both A and B flights will play out their matches by the specified dates from May to August at a mutually agreed date, but no later than 14 days between matches, excepting Wednesday. Should competitors be unable to agree to a mutually acceptable date to complete their match within the 14 day time frame, the winner will be decided by coin toss (Note 2). If, during the playoff between the winners of Flights A and B, the player from Flight A wins, the championship is decided. If the player from Flight B wins, a second match must be played which will then decide the winner. Playoff rounds are to be completed within 14 days of the completion of play of both flights, but at a mutually agreed date, excepting Wednesdays. All ties to be played off hole by hole until one side wins (RCGA Rules of Golf, Rule 33-6, and Appendix I, Section 11).

The Midsummer Medal

Donated: In 1969

Rules of Play: Match play with current handicaps and played over four 18-hole rounds as scheduled. Ties to be broken by extra holes. (RCGA Rules of Golf 33-6 and Appendix I, Section 11)

In the event that all matches do not get completed in the scheduled four weeks, final matches shall be played on mutually agreed dates, same as in the Gamble Cup. Weekend players are welcome to compete. They will play one another on the weekend preceding the scheduled Wednesday matches, until one player is left undefeated. That player will then be slotted in to the Wednesday groupings and will have to arrange times to play. For members who do not wish to play in this event and for those knocked out, Wednesday play will be regular golf. In order to award weekly prizes for low gross, low net, putts, and to have rounds count towards the Average Low Gross, Average Low Net, Putting Championship, and Points Race, all holes must be fully played out, and all strokes recorded. For the Match results, a player may concede a hole, or "give" his opponent a putt, but cannot pick up the ball until it is holed out.

The Club Championship Trophy

Donated: In 1929 by Mr. A. G. Fredricks

Rules of Play: Power carts may be used in all flights. Stroke play only over 54 holes as scheduled. This competition is open to the top grouping of players whose handicaps approximate the lowest one-third of the members, and who have played a minimum of one-half of the scheduled Men's Club tournaments. Weekend members are required to play this tournament on Wednesday only. Ties will be broken by an 18-hole playoff within seven days of the completion of the third round as scheduled by the Executive Committee. Should competitors still be tied after this round a winner will be decided by playing off hole by hole (RCGA Rules of Golf Rule 33-6 and Appendix I, Section 11).

As this cup has the most significance to the club some additional history has *been included.*

From the earliest time on record, being 1929, the Championship had always been under the guidance of the 'Parent Division'. The Club Championship and Steward Trophy were played on the same day, Saturday or Sunday, for 3 consecutive weeks. Competition was to be <u>Medal Play</u>. Low gross wins the Championship, Low net wins the Steward Cup.

In 1979 the 1st Men's Division was formed. In a vote it was moved and passed that the Club Championship would continue to be played as previously, under the guidance of the Parent Division.

In 1980 it was voted in to modify the Club Championship, wherein, it was to be played over 3 weekends, separate from the Steward Cup, which is to be played as a 36 hole tournament, 2 -18 hole rounds over 2 consecutive weekends at the same time as the club championship.

In 1984 a new trophy was added necessitating a new format of play. The 'Beaton Trophy' was donated by Mr. Don Beaton in memory of his father Les, to be used for a new 'C' Flight in the competition.

New format as follows;

Qualifying Round – all players to qualify, gross scores to be used to set up flights. There are to be 3 flights, break down as follows:

'A' Flight (Championship) – 4 lowest gross scores, plus all ties qualify

'B' Flight (Steward Cup) – next 8 lowest gross scores, plus all ties,

'C' Flight (Beaton Trophy) – balance of entries.

Each Flight to play 3 rounds in addition to qualifying round to complete the tournament using the Medal Play format.

Championship Flight to be on the gross score only, no handicap. 'B'+'C' Flights to be on net score, gross score less handicap.

All rounds are to be played between dates posted for each round.

'B'+'C' Flights are to use up to date handicaps, which are frozen after the first round, and are to be used for all 3 rounds.

Rules – the standard rules of Golf and Course Rules shall apply to all 3 flights.

In 1986 a vote was taken, moved and passed, that the club championship be played as 'Match Play' format, rather than medal play, starting after the qualifying round.

And finally, in 1997 a vote was again taken, moved and passed, that the club championship be played as 'Medal Play' format, the same as it originally started many years before.

In 2002 a new trophy was added. The 'Archie McCulloch Memorial'. The winner of this trophy will be determined from the lowest net score achieved by the competitors playing in all 3 venues.

That is how the Championship has been played up to the present day, 2009.

The Steward Cup

Donated: In 1960 by Mr. Arthur Steward.

Rules of Play: To be used as the "Handicap Championship Cup". Stroke play with handicaps frozen over 54 holes. This competition will run concurrent with the championship flight and is open to those players whose handicaps approximate the middle grouping of the members, and who have played a minimum of one-half of the Men's Club tournaments. Weekend members are required to play this tournament on Wednesday only. Ties will be broken by an 18-hole playoff within seven days of the completion of the third round as scheduled by the Executive Committee. Should a tie continue to exist after this round the winner will be determined by playing off hole by hole (RCGA Rules of Golf, Rule 33-6 and Appendix I, Section 11). First cup winner was Mr. Sutherland in 1960

The Beaton Trophy

Donated: In 1984 by Don Beaton in memory of his father Mr. Les Beaton.

Rules of Play: Trophy is to be used for the 'C' Flight of the Club Championship. Stroke play with handicaps frozen over 54 holes. This competition will run concurrent with the championship flight and is open to those members whose handicaps approximate the third highest handicap grouping of the members, and who have played a minimum of one-half of the Men's Club tournaments. Weekend members are required to play this tournament on Wednesday only. Ties will be broken by an 18-hole playoff within seven days of the completion of the third round as scheduled by the Executive Committee. Should a tie continue to exist after this round the winner will be determined by playing off hole by hole (RCGA Rules of Golf, Rule 33-6 and Appendix I, Section 11).

The McCulloch Memorial Net Champion Trophy

Donated: In 2002
Rules of Play: To be played in conjunction with the Club Championship, the Steward Cup, the Beaton Trophy. The winner of this trophy will be determined from the lowest net score achieved by the competitors playing in all 3 venues.

The Fall Cup

Donated: In 1945 by Mrs. G. A. Wilson
Rules of Play: Stroke play with current handicaps at time of play. Two 18-hole rounds as scheduled. Best net score will determine the winner. Ties will be broken by an 18 hole playoff within seven days of completion of the second round. Should competitors still be tied after this round a winner will be decided by playing off hole by hole (RCGA Rules of Golf, Rule 33-6 and Appendix I, Section 11)

The Cape Breton Trophy

Donated: In 1999 by Mr. D. Payne. (Note: The trophy was made by the crew of H.M.C.S. Cape Breton, and was originally a Labatt Beer curling trophy
Rules of Play: Stroke play with current handicaps at time of play. Two 18-hole rounds as scheduled. Best net score will determine the winner. Ties will be broken by

an 18 hole playoff within seven days of completion of the second round. Should competitors still be tied after this round a winner will be decided by playing off hole by hole (RCGA Rules of Golf, Rule 33-6 and Appendix I, Section 11) Weekend players are urged to complete their rounds on the preceding Sunday but no later than the following Sunday.

The John Plant Challenge

Donated: In 2003 to replace the button match trophies which are no longer played for.

Rules of Play: Two man Teams, (starting handicaps within 5 strokes) Round Robin Format, to be played from April 15 to Sept 15. Each team will play opponent teams twice, once match play, once stroke play, using the average team handicap at time of play. Matches are to be played in 18 straight holes (no 2 nine hole matches, Exception to the Nine Hole men's Club.) Team Handicaps cannot go above a 5 point spread. If so, higher handicap player must go down to a 5 point spread. Two points for a win, one point for a tie. Two dollar entry fee per person. Contestants are eligible to play in next years Green & Hay tournament.

The Rob Butler Memorial

Donated: In 2006 by the Men's Division. Originally just called the Putting Championship trophy, renamed in 2009 following the death of Mr. Rob Butler, who loved this competition and often "played for putts".

Rules of Play: Best Putter Trophy: To be awarded to the player with the lowest putts per hole average through-out the season. Players must record putts for each hole on Men's Day. Results will be tabulated an winner

du Temple *and* Ostachowicz

announced at season's end. Only those members who have completed two-thirds of the Men's Club regularly scheduled tournaments/competitions are eligible to compete for this award.

The Seasons Points Champion

Donated: In 2007 by Tom Collett
Rules of Play: A Points Race, affectionately called the FED-UP cup (as in the PGA Fed-ex cup), with points awarded weekly based on net scores. Players are ranked, and points awarded. Ties will split the points. At the end of the year cash prizes will be awarded to the top two total points winners.

The Winter Eclectic

Donated: In 1997
Rules of Play: Match Play with current handicaps (until frozen) for the duration of the tournament. The winner will be determined from the highest number of points earned (Win: 2 points/Tie: 1 point/Loss: 0); the winner of the Winter Eclectic will be determined from the Low Net scores in the respective handicap categories of 0-20 and 21 plus. The player with the overall Low Gross score in the Winter Eclectic will be awarded the Winter Low Gross Trophy. Ties for low gross and low net scores will be broken by one 18-hole play off. All games are based on 18 consecutive holes and must be played with another Men's Club member only. Should play be halted due to inclement weather and/or darkness, and at least nine holes have been played, the remaining nine holes must be played within ten days providing another 18 holes have not been played in between. If the second nine holes cannot be played within the ten-day period,

the round must be played over. When Temporary Holes are in play, scores on these holes are not to be counted for the Eclectic

The A.H. Donald Perpetual Cup Winter Round Robin

Donated: In 1960
Rules of Play: This is a 'Match Play' competition with current handicaps. 2 Points are awarded to the player winning the most number holes. In the event of a tie both players receive 1 point.

The Mudder Four Club

Donated: In 2008, and hand crafted by Mr. C. Turner
Rules of Play: Played using Three clubs and a putter only, stroke play.

The Green and Hay Trophy

Donated: In 1955
Rules of Play: The format and dates of play will be set by the John Plant Challenge coordinators. The format is usually stroke play with current handicaps at time of play over two 18-hole rounds. This competition is open only to those members who participated in the John Plant challenge matches. Rounds are to be played outside of the scheduled Men's Day on mutually agreed dates. Entrants may play their two rounds on any given day, but must declare to their playing partner(s) , before teeing off, that this will be a Green & Hay round.

The Captains Trophy

Donated: In 2009, and hand crafted by Mr. C. Turner

Rules of Play: This trophy is competed for by the current men's division executive, and other players who formerly served on the Club Executive.

The Most Improved Player Plaque

Donated: In 1996 by Mr. Murray Matheson
Rules of Play: The player with the highest improvement factor over the season will receive the most improved golfer award (RCGA Handicap Manual, Appendix H) . Only those members who have completed two-thirds of the Men's Club regularly scheduled tournaments/competitions are eligible to compete for this award.

The Average Low Gross and Low Net Trophy

Donated: In 1984 BY Mr. Joe Flint
Rules of Play: For the best Low Gross + Low Net scoring average throughout the year on Men's Days. Only those members having completed two-thirds of the Men's Club regularly scheduled tournaments/competitions are eligible to compete for this award.

The Silver and Bronze Button Matches

Donated: Buttons originally in 1930. New plaques were bought and buttons inserted in 2002.
NOTE: In 2007, competition is suspended. Replaced by the John Plant Challenge.
Former Rules of Play: 2 levels of play – The Silver Buttons: handicap of 0 – 18.
The Bronze Buttons: handicap of 19 – and over. Competitions are played in 2 man teams, played in Match Play format. Holes are won or lost using the lowest score on each hole from each team. All players play off the

lowest handicap player in the match. Competitions are played by challenges. A match must be played within 3 weeks of challenge. If not, buttons are forfeited to the challengers. If challengers do not play they are dropped to the bottom of the list. If there are a lot of challenges the time frame for playing may be reduced as determined by the club captain. Players must be within the handicap range of the button being played for. When a button holders handicap increases or decreases into the other handicap range, he must forfeit his button to the club championship. His partner may get another partner, but must play a match, and win, to get the button. When a challengers handicap increases or decreases, he must drop out of the challenge list. His partner may pick another partner, and maintain his position on the challenge board.

Men's 9-Hole Division' Events

The Nine Hole Championship

<u>Donated</u>: In 1994
<u>Rules of Play</u>: Stroke play only over 54 holes. Ties will be broken by an 18-hole playoff within seven days of the completion of the third round as scheduled by the Executive Committee. Should competitors still be tied after this round a winner will be decided by playing off hole by hole (RCGA Rules of Golf Rule 33-6 and Appendix I, Section 11).

The Nine Hole Aggregate Low Net

<u>Donated</u>: In 1988

Rules of Play: Best low net score accumulated through-out the years play.

The Ladies Division Events

The Spring Trophy

Donated: In 1977

Rules of Play: 18-Hole competition with a Qualifying Round to be stroke play on handicap. To be followed by three 18-Hole Match play rounds. Draw in accordance with RCGA Rules of Golf. In the case of a tie another round must be played, continuing to sudden death if required.

Spring Trophy: Best eight net scores of all players in qualifying round.

Spring Cup: Next eight best net scores.

The Spring Cup – Second Flight

Donated: In 1977

Rules of Play: 18-Hole competition, with a Qualifying Round to be stroke play on handicap. To be followed by three 18-Hole Match play rounds. Draw in accordance with RCGA Rules of Golf. In the case of a tie another round must be played, continuing to sudden death if required.

Spring Trophy: Best eight net scores of all players in qualifying round.

Spring Cup: Next eight best net scores.

The Handicap Reduction Award Plaque

Donated: In 1993 by Miss Penny Basiuk (du Temple) to replace the original one that was retired.

Rules of Play: Must have an established handicap. Must post a minimum of 20 games in the current calendar year. Follows the guidelines of the Provincial Ladies Golf Association to compute the winner.

The Steward Bowl

Donated: In 1965

Rules of Play: This is the Winter Round Robin award. To be played as 9-hole match play games during the off season. Scoring: plus for a win; minus for a loss; zero for a tie. At the end points are totaled: two points for a win; one point for a tie. In case of a tie the player with the most pluses wins, if still tied an additional round is played, continuing to sudden death if required.

The Du Temple Memorial Cup

Donated: In 1964 by the duTemple family in memory of Mr. George duTemple.

Rules of Play: 18-hole medal play, using the 2 ball format. Each player plays own game, but records best score on each hole from the partnership. Total the score and deduct one-half the lower handicap. Low net score wins. In case of a tie another full round is played, continuing to sudden death if required.

The Ladies Championship

Donated: In 1939 by the Ardmore Golf Club

Rules of Play: This is an 18-hole medal play format competition. Players must have played in five Tuesday morning Ladies Day games or other designated Ladies Division events. There is no qualifying round. Members are placed in flights based on handicap factors at start of play. The eight players with the lowest factors play the Championship Flight. Remaining players are divided equally between Silver and Bronze Flights. All three flights will play a total of three consecutive 18-hole rounds using gross scores. In case of a tie for winner or runner-up, another full round is played, continuing to sudden death if required.

National Award for Club Championship "Net Winner" (C.L.G.A.) – This is a Nationally sponsored pin presented to the lowest aggregate of the three net scores in all three flights of the Club Championship. If the low net winner is also the low gross winner she is entitled to this pin. In the case of 'Match Play' format, the low net score of the qualifying round is used.

The Ladies Championship Second Flight

Donated: In 1970

Rules of Play: This is an 18-hole medal play format competition. Players must have played in five Tuesday morning Ladies Day games or other designated Ladies Division events. There is no qualifying round. Members are placed in flights based on handicap factors at start of play. The eight players with the lowest factors play the Championship Flight. Remaining players are divided equally between Silver and Bronze Flights. All three flights will play a total of three consecutive 18-hole rounds using gross scores. In case of a tie for winner or runner-up, another full round is played, continuing to sudden death if required.

National Award for Club Championship "Net Winner" (C.L.G.A.) This is a Nationally sponsored pin presented to the lowest aggregate of the three net scores in all three flights of the Club Championship. If the low net winner is also the low gross winner she is entitled to this pin. In the case of 'Match Play' format, the low net score of the qualifying round is used.

The Ladies Championship Third Flight

<u>Donated</u>: In 1973 by Isobel and Len Valentine.

<u>Rules of Play</u>: This is an 18-hole medal play format competition. Players must have played in five Tuesday morning Ladies Day games or other designated Ladies Division events. No qualifying round. Members placed in flights based on handicap factors at start of play. The eight players with the lowest factors play the Championship Flight. Remaining players are divided equally between Silver and Bronze Flights. All three flights will play a total of three consecutive 18-hole rounds using gross scores. In case of a tie for winner or runner-up, another full round is played, continuing to sudden death if required.

National Award for Club Championship "Net Winner" (C.L.G.A.) – This is a Nationally sponsored pin presented to the lowest aggregate of the three net scores in all three flights of the Club Championship. If the low net winner is also the low gross winner she is entitled to this pin. In the case of 'Match Play' format, the low net score of the qualifying round is used.

The Valentine Rose Bowl

<u>Donated</u>: In 1991 by Isabel Valentine in memory of her husband Len.

<u>Rules of Play</u>: To replace the Margaret Rose Trophy. Play to remain using the original format. An 18-hole medal play (stroke play) format. Players record 5 rounds of play, best three rounds are tabulated. Best net score

wins. In case of a tie for winner or runner-up, another full round is played, continuing to sudden death if required.

The Mutual Auto Sales

Donated: In 1939

Rules of Play: Used for the Par Competition. Played in conjunction with C.L.G.A. games, using five rounds during the year, plus a play-off. 18-hole, stroke play, using full handicap to calculate par for each hole to determine scoring. That being a (+), (-), or (0) for that hole. *E.g. A players par on a hole (using the handicap) is 6, she scores a 5 giving her a (+), if she scores 6 she gets a (0), if she scores 7 she gets a (-). Rounds are tabulated and plus and minuses totaled. If a player has 7 pluses and 5 minuses, the result is Plus 2(+2).* Each Par day the players with the three best scores are listed on a chart, regardless that they may already be listed. When five rounds are completed the players listed are eligible to compete in the Par playoff. In case of a tie another full round is played, continuing to sudden death if required.

The Emily Young low Net Award

Donated: In 1964 2001.

Rules of Play: This award goes to the player having the lowest net average in competitions played throughout the season, determined by calculating the total number of individual rounds played and averaging it among the number of players taking part. This figure is used as the minimum number of rounds for a member to be eligible for the award. Individual averages are then determined with the lowest net winning.

The J. J. White Cup

Donated: In 1929 by Mr. and Mrs. J.J. White to the North Saanich Golf Club.

Rules of Play: Competition is medal (Stroke) play on handicap, with two 18-hoole round on consecutive Tuesdays. The two net scores are added with low net winning. In case of a tie another full round is played, continuing to sudden death if required.

The Ladies Putting Award

Donated: In 1999 by Mrs. Jean Streeter

Rules of Play: Award to be presented to the best putter throughout the golf season on Ladies Day play. Played in conjunction with the five Valentine Rose Bowl games. Best three games of five, lowest total of putts.

ADDITIONAL COMPETITIONS

Dorthy Olive Franklin Tournement

A Provincial 18-hole tournament played at the club level on a regular Ladies Day. Established to honor the memory of Dorthy Franklin, a highly regarded member from Point Grey Golf Club in Vancouver, serving many years on the BC and Canadian Executive Boards. Tournament is combined with any stroke play competition normally schedule in the month of June.

Participation is voluntary and played are to pay a minimal entry fee, with funds going to the Zone for Junior Girls Golf Programs and to assist with Junior Team's travel.

At Club Level winning and runner-up players with Low Net scores are awarded balls. Scores submitted to the Zone are eligible to be the Provincial winner.

Eclectic Competitions

These are 9-hole competitions where 18-hole players may use score from both nine rounds. Only rounds played with regular Tuesday morning draw may be used. Players are divided into two handicap groups at the Captain discretion. Members record their best scores for each hole during stipulated time period. When final core are entered, the eclectic committee total the scores to determine the Low Gross of each player, then subtracts one-quarter the handicap to determine the Low Net. At the end of each competition gross and net prizes are awarded.

Captain vs. Secretary Competition

A fun Team Competition using Match Play format on handicap. Players draw from two sets of buttons (one color for the Captain and the other for the secretary), or by assigning numbers as names are drawn (odds and evens), or any other method at the discretion of the Captain.

Player winning the most holes in the first nine receives 1 point, in the second nine 1 point, plus over the 18 holes gets I point. Ties get one-half point each. Team with the most points win. No prizes awarded. Winning team players buy their opponents a small treat, such as coffee, a chocolate bar, or a bag of tees.

Pender Island vs. Ardmore Interclub

First play in 1979. A plaque was purchased in 1984 with the cost shared by both clubs. Clubs arrange dates yearly, one game at Pender and one game at Ardmore.

Effective 1994, only eight players from each club take part. Players should be the same for both matches.

It is an 18-hole, stroke play competition, on handicap. Eight Net scores from each Cub, at both visits are recorded. Team with the lowest score wins the plaque. Individual Low Gross, and Low Net winners, and the player with least putts are awarded prizes.

When there are more entries than required the team is selected using the eight best Net scores from a previous Tuesday game.

Cowichan vs. Ardmore Interclub

First played in 1952. Clubs arrange dates yearly, one game at Cowichan and one game at Ardmore. Players should be available for both matches. Eight players from each club take part. Ladies with similar handicaps compete against each other.

This is an 18-hole, best-ball Match play competition, on handicaps. In each foursome two players from each club play as a team using the best Net score to determine the winner of each hole. Strokes are taken from the lowest handicap of the foursome. Winning team of each hole is awarded one point for their club while a tie counts as one-half point for each team. Points are totaled over the two matches to determine the overall winning club.

There is no trophy, cup, or prizes for this competition.

When there are more entries than required the team is selected using the eight best Net scores from a previous Tuesday game.

Audrey Benn Button Matches

Two Silver Buttons were donated in 1995 by Mrs. Audrey Benn, a Club Member. Competition to be 18-hole Match play to be ongoing year round. The Buttons are held by the current winners until challenged and lost.

Players choose a partner and challenge the button holders. There should no more
Than seven strokes difference in handicaps between teams. Strokes given are calculated by totaling each team's handicap and taking the difference of the totals. e.g.,

Team 'A'	Team 'B'
Hdcp 20	Hdcp 28
Hdcp 38	Hdcp 36
58	64

(Team 'A' gives Team 'B' six strokes.)

Each player plays own game. After each hole, strokes of each tam are totaled and adjusted by strokes given under handicaps, to determine the low score and winner of the hole (+,-,0). The pair with most pluses wins the match. Losing pair wishing to re-challenge must find new partners or wait until another pair has challenged and played. Matches tie after 18 hole are decided by sudden death.

Winners and challengers names are entered on the designated list on the bulletin board. Date of challenge should be recorded, and must be game completed within one week. Challenged Button holders must comply with the challenge within two weeks they forfeit the buttons. If challengers cannot comply they must remove their names allowing new challengers to sign up. If a button holder will be absent for a period longer than two weeks she must surrender the button and her partner can take a new partner.

If while holding the Buttons, handicaps of the Button Holders change, they must continue play through matches using their current handicaps, even when their handicap difference become less than the specifies seven strokes.

Fun Games

Big Five

18-hole Competition – Handicaps – Stroke Play
Points Given For:
1 point for reaching green I "regulation" – i.e.
1 stroke on par 3
2 strokes on par 4
3 strokes on par 5
2 points for 1 putt
3 points for holing-in from off the green
4 points for holing-in from sand trap
5 points for hole-in-one.
All ties honored with a prize

Honey Pot

18 Hole Competition using handicaps as follows:
If handicap is 28, subtract 18 from 28, leaving 10 – this means the player would be allowed two strokes on 10 holes and one stroke on remaining holes. If handicap is more than 36, they would receive three strokes on the appropriate holes and two on every other hole.
Points: 1 for bogey, 2 for par, 3 for birdie, 4 for eagle, 5 for hole-in-one
All ties honored with a prize

Criers Tournament

Following 18 holes of stroke play, competitors change the score o each of their four worst holes to pars before adding their scores. These holes can be four overall or two from each nine at the discretion of the Captain. A when scores are totaled, deduct handicap and the player with the lowest net score is the winner. If playing a nine hole competition, change the scores on two holes only and deduct one half of the handicap.

Name Your Score

Nine-Hole or 18-Hole Competition at the Captain's discretion.

Before commencing play each competitor advises the captain of what gross score they predict they will shoot. The winner is the player whose score is closest to their prediction.

Fairways and Greens

Nine or eighteen-hole competition at the Captain's discretion.

Players receive one point each time that their tee shot comes to rest on the closely mown portion of the fairway, except on par threes. On the par threes there are no points for coming to rest on the fairway but the player receives two points if their tee shot comes to rest on the green.

The winner is the player receiving the highest number of points.

Half & Half

18-hole competition

First nine holes, player uses total putts.

Second nine holes, player uses strokes minus $\frac{1}{2}$ handicap.

Add total putts and the second nine score – this determines the final score.

Low score wins.

Tombstone (Flag) Competition

18-hole Competition.

Each player is given a small flag or wooden stake on which she writes her name and the total of par plus her handicap strokes. When the player has used that number of strokes she "plants" her flag where the ball rests. If in a hazard or o a green, the flag should be planted at the edge. The player whose flag is the furthest advanced is declared the winner. If after completing 18 holes, players still have strokes remaining, to break the tie they may begin a second round, proceeding until all of their strokes are used. Alternately the Captain may determine the winner(s) according to the number of unused strokes after 18 holes.

Hidden Hole

18-hole stroke play.

The Captain asks a non-player, usually someone from the Pro Shop, to put two numbers in an envelope, one for the first nine holes and one for the second nine holes. Everyone draws and plays their own game. After the game, the Captain or Vice-Captain opens the envelope. The players subtract the score of the hidden holes from their score and deduct their handicap.

Throw Out Two

Following 18 holes of stroke play, competitors throw out the scores on their two worst holes before adding the scores. These holes can be two overall or one from each nine at the discretion of the Captain. When scores are totaled, deduct the handicap and the player with the lowest net score is the winner. A nine-hole competition is played as "Throw Out One" with a deduction of one half the handicap.

T. and F. Fun Competition

18 Hole Competition
Circle holes that start with "T" and "F", numbering as First, Second, Third etc. Total all circled holes and deduct handicap.
Tie Break at the discretion of Captain.

Yellow Ball

Team of four players. Each team is given a yellow ball as the Team Ball.

Before commencing play, teams will decide by lot, such as tossing tees, the order in which they will play for the team (#1, 2, 3 or 4), keeping this order throughout . If playing in a threesome, the order of play should be changed for the second nine.

Players each play their own game but, in the order decided upon, will take turns using the yellow ball instead of their own ball on that particular hole and their score on that hole will be the Team score. (On each hole it will be someone's turn to use the yellow ball.) If the yellow ball is lost, another clearly marked ball should be substituted. Teams losing the yellow ball will have two penalty strokes added to their team score at the end of play.

To determine the team handicap, total individual handicaps and average. Since the handicaps are averaged this game also can be played with threesomes or even twosomes. If only playing nine holes use one-half of the team handicap.

Golf balls will be awarded to the team with the lowest net score plus individual low gross and low net.

Scramble

N.B. This format established by Ladies Club

Nine Hole Competition, Teams of four.

Each player drives. Players decide which of the drives they wish to use and a marker is placed on that spot. The other team members then pick up their balls and hit from the marked spot. A player cannot hit two consecutive shots until they reach the green. All four players may putt. (Similar to a four-ball-onesome)

Each person's drive must be used two times. One hole is optional a any time and any of the players drives may be used for this optional hole.

Total the four handicaps and divide by four for net score.

Threesome:

When there are three players in a group, each members drive will be used three times and each member will hit the ball every stroke. Handicaps will be totaled and divided by three.

Four-Ball Best-Ball

Eighteen hole stoke play, team competition.

Participants are divided into two handicap divisions using two from each division to make up the foursomes. Players each play their own game applying individual full handicaps.

The low net score on each hole is used as the team score. Team with the lowest net is the winner.

To figure out the player's par (how many strokes they receive on each hole), subtract 18 from their handicap. This gives the number of holes on which they receive 2 strokes. On the balance of the holes they receive one stroke.

Coloured photographs of all the trophies presently in use and also of those that are now archived can be viewed on the website of Ardmore Golf Course at: www. ardmoregolfcourse.com

Appendix B

Presidents and Vice-Presidents

Year	Presidents	Vice-Presidents
1934	Mr. J.J. White	Mr. G. F. Pownall
1935	Mr. J.J. White	Mr. J.C. Anderson
1936	Mr. .J.J. White	Mr. G.F. Pownall
1937	Mr. G. F. Pownall	Mr. F.J. Baker
1938	Mr. G. F. Pownall	Mr. F.J. Baker
1939	Mr. F.J. Baker	Mr. J.C. Anderson
1940	Mr. C. D. Eves	Mr. P.A. Bodkin
1941	Mr. J.C. Anderson	Mr. P.A. Bodkin
1942	Mr. P.A. Bodkin	Mr. F.J. Baker
1943	Mr. P.A. Bodkin	Mr. F.J. Baker
1944	Mr. P.A. Bodkin	Mr. F.J. Baker
1945	Mr. P.A. Bodkin	Mr. F.J. Baker
1946	Mr. P.A. Bodkin	Major W.E. Tayler
1947	Mr. J. C. Anderson,	Mr. G. Watt
1948	Mr. J. C. Anderson.	Mr. Clay
1949	Mr. J. C. Burbidge	Major G. Smith
1950	Mr. J. C. Burbidge	Major G. Smith
1951	Mr. A. H. Griffiths	Mr. E.W. Townsend
1952	Mr. A. H. Griffiths	Mr. H.E. Kennedy
1953	Mr. V. E. Virgin	Mr. Currell
1954	Mr. V. E. Virgin	Mr. R.S. Bunyard
1955	Mr. J.C. Anderson	Mr. E.W. Townsend
1956	Mr. A.C. Foreman	Mr. E.W. Townsend
1957	Mr. A.C. Foreman	Mr. J. Sim
1958	Capt. J. Barr	Mr. D. McLellan

1959	Capt. J. Barr	Mr. D. McLellan
1960	Mr. J. Bendal	Mr. D. McLellan
1961	Mr. B. duTemple	Mr. A. Steward
1962	Mr. B. du Temple	Mr. E. Vickerman
1963	Mr. B. du Temple	Mr. J. McKnight
1964	Mr. B. du Temple	Mr. N. Camsusa
1965	Mr. F. Dutton	Mr. D. Scott
1966	Mr. F. Dutton	Mr. D. Scott
1967	Mr. F. Dutton	Mr. A.S. Spreight
1968	Mr. F. Dutton	Mr. A.S. Spreight
1969	Mr. F. Dutton	Mr. A.S. Spreight
1970	Mr. F. Dutton	Mr. E. Vickerman
1971	Mr. E. Vickerman	Mr. H. Pelton
1972	Mr. E. Vickerman	Mr. C. Hilton
1973	Mr. E. Vickerman	Mr. C. Hilton
1974	Mr. E. Vickerman	Mr. C. Hilton
1975	Mrs. B. Clement	Mrs. G. Jones
1976	Mrs. B. Clement	Mrs. G. Jones
1977	Mr. C.W. Speers	Mr. L. Valentine
1978	Mr. L. Valentine	Mr. G. Kaiser
1979	MR. L.Valentine	Mr. G. Kaiser
1980	Mr. G. Kaiser	Mr. A. Rowbottom
1981	Mrs. E. Larter	Mr. F. Loveless
1982	Mr. F. Loveless	Mrs. I. Clarke
1983	Mrs. I. Clarke	Mr. B. Watson
1984	Mr. B. Watson	Mrs. E. Williams
1985	Mrs. E. Williams	Mr. P. Bishop
1986	Mr. P. Williams	Mrs. B. Harmon
1987	Mrs. B. Harmon	Mr. F. Emmerson
1988	Mr. F. Emmerson	Mrs. D. Emmerson
1989	Mr. E. Airey	Mrs. E. Williams
1990	Mr. E. Airey	Mrs. E. Williams
1991	Mr. P. Bishop	Mr. G. Smashnuk
1992	Mr. G. Smashnuk	Mrs. J. Toller

Presidents and Vice-Presidents

1993 . . . . Mrs. J. Toller . . . . Mr. G. Shute

1994 . . . . Mr. G. Shute . . . . . . Mr. E.R. Ostachowicz

1995 . . . . . . Mr. E. Ostachowicz . . . . Mr. D. Payne

1996 . . . . . . Mr. E. Ostachowicz . . . . .Mr. D. Scott

1997 . . . . . . Mr. E. Ostachowicz . . . . Mr. R. Butler

1998 . . . . .Mr. R Butler . . . . Mrs. J.Toller

1999 . . . . Mrs. J. Toller . . . . Mr. C. King

2000 . . . . .Mr. E. Airey. . . . . Mrs. E Jordan

2001 . . . . .Mrs. E Jordan. . . . . Mr. D. Lachmund

2002. . . . . .Mrs. E Jordan. . . . . Mr. D. Lachmund

2003. . . . . . Mr. E. Ostachowicz . . . . . . Mr. D. Lachmund

2004. . . . . . Mr. E. Ostachowicz . . . . . . Mr. D. Lachmund

2005. . . . . . . Mr. D. Lachmund . . . . . . .Mrs. B. Danbrook

2006. . . . . . . Mr. D. Lachmund . . . . Mr. J. Hill

2007. . . . . . . Mr. D. Lachmund . . . . Mr. J. Hill

2008. . . . . Mr. S. Sam . . . . .Mr. C.Tom

Appendix C

Club Championship Ladies

1939	Mrs. Sisson
1940	Mrs. Sisson
1941	Miss. Fraser
1947	Miss. Gwynne
1948	Mrs. H. Horth
1949	Miss. Paynter
1950	Mrs. Sisson
1951	Mrs. E.W. Townsend
1952	Mrs. Sisson
1953	Mrs. E.W. Townsend
1954	Mrs. Sisson
1955	Mrs. F.S. Green
1956	Mrs. G.L. Hay
1957	Mrs. Sisson
1958	Mrs. Sisson
1959	Mrs. Vickerman
1960	Mrs. J. H. Wilson
1961	Miss M. Haynes
1962	Mrs. F.S. Green
1963	Mrs. R. G. du Temple
1964	Mrs. R. G. du Temple
1965	Mrs. R. G. du Temple
1966	Mrs. Sisson
1967	Mrs. R. G. du Temple
1968	Mrs. R. G. du Temple
1969	Mrs. R. G. du Temple

Club Championship Ladies

1970	Mrs. R. G. du Temple
1971	Mrs. R. G. du Temple
1972	Mrs. A. Clemett
1973	Miss. T. Elmsley
1974	Miss. T. Elmsley
1975	Miss. T. Elmsley
1976	Mrs. R. Cole
1977	Mrs. R. Cole
1978	Mrs. R. Cole
1979	Mrs. R. Cole
1980	Miss T. Elmsley
1982	Mrs. L. Petrie
1983	Mrs. L. Petrie
1984	Mrs. L. Petrie
1985	M. Jerome
1986	S. Hayes
1987	L. Clarke
1988	L. Clarke
1989	T. Henderson
1990	J. Toller
1991	J. Toller
1992	J. Toller
1993	J. Toller
1994	A. Benn
1995	J. Toller
1996	S. Hayes
1997	C. Hemphill
1998	C. Hemphill
1999	C. Hemphill
2000	C. Hemphill
2001	L. Worsley
2002	L. Worsley

2003	C. Jones
2004	L. Worsley
2005	L. Worsley
2006	S. Page
2007	L. Pengelly
2008	L. Pengelly
2009	L. Worsley
2010	A. Hawkins
2011	A. Hawkins

Club Championship Men

1929 . . . . P. Hope
1930 . . . . P. Hope
1931 . . . . P. Hope
1932 . . . . W.T. Sisson
1933 . . . . P. Hope
1934 . . . . A. Deildal
1935 . . . . J. McIlraith
1936 . . . . W.T. Sisson
1937 . . . . J. C. Anderson
1938 . . . . .A . Deildal
1939 . . . . A. Deildal
1940 . . . . J.C. Anderson
1941 . . . . .F.A. Urquhart
1945 . . . . B.L. Forster
1946 . . . . .F.A. Urquhart
1947 . . . . J.C. Anderson
1948 . . . . .F.A. Urquhart
1949 . . . . John Watt
1950 . . . . .F.A. Urquhart
1951 . . . . .J.M. Brooks
1952 . . . . A.W. Brownlie
1953 . . . . Wally G. du Temple
1954 . . . . Wally G. du Temple
1955 . . . . .Arch C. Foreman
1956 . . . . .Gordon L. Hay
1957 . . . . Wally G. du Temple
1958 . . . . Wally G. du Temple
1959 . . . . Wally G. du Temple
1960 . . . . Wally G. du Temple
1961 . . . . .H. Jacobsen
1962 . . . . T. Mehew
1963 . . . . .H. Jacobsen

Year	Winner
1964	E. Beauchemin
1965	H. Jacobsen
1966	E. Beauchemin
1967	E. Beauchemin
1968	H. Pelton
1969	F. Dutton
1970	H. Pelton
1971	K. Soles
1972	F. Dutton
1973	B. Hart
1974	G. Kurtz
1975	D. Dicks
1976	F. Tupper
1977	A. Pelton
1978	E. Ostachowicz
1979	R. Treleaven
1980	R. Treleaven
1981	R. Treleaven
1982	R. Treleaven
1983	B. Wright
1984	B. Wright
1985	E. Masson
1986	L. Meyers
1987	G. Shute
1988	L. McCulloch
1989	J. Johnstone
1990	G. Laboucan
1991	E. Ostachowicz
1992	E. Ostachowicz
1993	B. Bingley
1994	E. Ostachowicz
1995	E. Ostachowicz
1996	E. Ostachowicz
1997	E. Ostachowicz

Club Championship Men

1998 . . . . K. McTaggart
1999 . . . . E. Ostachowicz
2000 . . . . .A. Pelton
2001 . . . . Reagan Pringle
2002. . . . . E. Ostachowicz
2003. . . . . .A. Pelton
2004. . . . . Rayny Day
2005. . . . . Rayny Day
2006. . . . . Rayny Day
2007. . . . . Rayny Day
2008. . . . . Rayny Day
2009. . . . . Rayny Day
2010 . . . . .I. Philp
2011. . . . . Rayny Day

Appendix D

The List of Life Members Honoured For
Meritorious Service

Bill, Robin,
Bradley, Herb,
Bradley, Zelma,
Bouteillier, Bob,
Bouteillier, Helen
Bowerman, Jack
Bowerman, Marjorie
Butler, Dan
Craik, Bob
Creak, Rose
De Jong, Greg
Fraser, Diana
Gardner, Ron
Gray, Ernie
Gwynne, Eveline
Johnson, George
Johnstone, Jim
Johnstone, May
Jolly, Ernie
Kurtz, Sid
Lee, Alison
McCulloch, Archie
McLeod, Bill
Mountfield, Harry
Ostachowicz, Edward
Stevens, Kent

Steward, Arthur
Steward, Doris
Trerise, Ted
Valentine, Len
Valentine, Isobel
Watson, Bill
Williams, Ethel
Yells, Reg

Selected Bibliography

NEWSPAPERS

The Victoria Province November 2nd 1895

The Review, March 20th 1985

The Peninsula News Review, May 18th 1949

The Peninsula And Gulf Islands Review, May 18th

ARCHIVAL RESOURCES

British Columbia Archives

Visual records, documents, audio-files

The Sidney Archives

The Saanich Pioneers' Society Archives

UNPUBLISHED

Ardmore Estate Sales Brochure, R. Cussack
Presses, Victoria

History of Holy Trinity Church 1885 - 1985

Notes collected from interviews by Edward
R. Ostachowicz

Notes collected from interviews by Wally G. du Temple

The Alice du Temple Memoir entitled "Memories, Then
and Later"

The Diaries of George Walter du Temple

The Notes of Barry G. du Temple

The Records of the North Saanich Golf Club

The Records of Ardmore Golf Club

The Records of Ardmore Golf Course Ltd.

PUBLICATIONS

Barclay, James A. *Golf In Canada, A History*, Toronto: McClelland and Stewart Inc., 1992

Bell, Betty. *The fair land, Saanich,* Victoria: Sono Nis Press, 1982

Bosher, J. F. *Imperial Vancouver Island,* USA: Xlibris Corporation, 2010

Coyle, Brendan. *War On Our Doorstep*, Surrey: Heritage House Publishing, 2002

Corley-Smith, Peter. *Victoria Golf Club 1893-1993*, Victoria: V.G.C. Centennial Committee, 1992

Grant, Peter. *The Story of Sidney,* Victoria: Porthole Press, 1998

Hern, Frances. *Amazing Stories, Yip Sang and the First Chinese Canadians,* Victoria: Heritage House Publishing Company Ltd, 2011

Horth, Nell. *North Saanich, Memories and Pioneers*, Sidney: Porthole Press Ltd,1988

Huck, Barbara. *In Search of Ancient British Columbia,* Winnipeg: Heartland, 2006

Jones, Bobby. *Bobby Jones on Golf*, New York: New Metropolitan, 1926

Matthew, Sidney L. *Bobby Jones Extra*, Florida: I.Q. Press, 2004

Muralt, Darryl E. *The Victoria and Sidney Railway*: Victoria: B. C. Railway Historical Association, 1992

Reksten, Terry. *More English Than The English*, Winlaw:Sono Nis Press, 2011

Teague, J. *John Dean Cabin Diary*, North Saanich: John Dean Nature House, 2009

Virgin, Victor E. *History of North Saanich and South Saanich, Pioneers and District,* Saanich: Saanich Pioneer Society

Electronic

Wikipedia.com

CPSIA information can be obtained
at www.ICGtesting.com
Printed in the USA
LVIW010811300912
300877LV00001B